# A COACH'S JOURNEY

## Discussing Essential Aspects and Lessons of Professional Coaching

### STEVE J. ANDERSON

*Tellwell Talent*
*www.tellwell.ca*

*ISBN*
*978-0-2288-2487-9 (Paperback)*
*978-0-2288-3181-5 (Ebook)*

# Table of Contents

# FOREWORD

Steve Anderson has committed his life to sport as an athlete, coach and administrator. His passion for the lessons sport teaches began as a young sportsman on Queensland's Central Highlands where he excelled in athletics while eventually pursuing rugby as his chosen sport.

Steve developed from player to club coach to coaching professional. His journey includes time in the National Rugby League with the Melbourne Storm when they won their first premiership as well as World Cups and rugby union high-performance appointments around the world. It is a coaching journey with many lessons learnt, many coaches to learn from and many anecdotes to share.

Steve's wisdom gained as player and coach prepared him well for senior roles in elite performance coaching. You can't take the coach out of the man. Steve is a coach who wants to positively influence young lives!

Steve is a good man, a man of integrity. He is a lifelong learner from the schools and universities of sport. He has played with the best, been coached by and worked with world-class coaches and graduated to the international level.

In this great book, Steve brings the voice of an elder to the pages. The words of wisdom are based on experiences, both good and bad, of athletes, coaches and administrators.

As you read you will learn about Steve's hard-earned and passionate commitment to sport and the life lessons it has taught him. As a sport elder, he now wants others walking in his footsteps to learn from his ongoing journey. You will read about character, values and standards set. You will read about integrity and belief in self. He shares these life lessons from sport now so younger athletes, coaches, administrators and lovers of sport will continue his work.

This collection of words and experiences has many lessons for all sport lovers. The book is an easy read. It's broken into logical sections with headings and sub-headings enabling you to read a logical flow of ideas, experiences and stories or simply pick up a section here and there that has meaning to you.

Above all, the book oozes the man himself. A man of character, wisdom and experience; a man of substance. A sport man. A sport elder. I hope you will enjoy the many life lessons Steve shares in this wonderful book as much as I enjoyed them.

- Peter Reaburn (professor and Head of Exercise and Sports Science at the Bond Institute of Health and Sport)

# PREFACE

Through a series of discussions, this book challenges common perceptions and shows the experiences of coaching. The subject matter has been specifically selected from twenty-five years of personal experience in professional coaching because it is uniquely suited to the modern coach in any sport. In this book I will:

- Provide a guide for aspiring and professional coaches that will foster individual thinking and drive personal development. I want to challenge the reader to think about and debate my opinions to enhance their personal development. My journey contains periods of doubt that hindered my growth, and I will use these times to discuss how I got past them. After twenty-five years I still grapple with doubt, although now I manage it much better through experience. Accepting self-doubt as part of coaching is presented as fundamental to learning.
- Ensure that coaching is considered as a derivative of your personality, and that observing, researching and sourcing information and methodology provides a continuous learning approach to your development. Learning is presented as a means of self-realisation in coaching. Confidence appears fragmented in my early development largely due to inability to manage the many and varied dynamics of coaching.
- Present that failure has many facets that are out of your control. To rationalise failure is to accept winning and losing as equally

important when considering success. Success has many forms
that change as experience nurtures perception and the realities
of being the coach.

This book presents four sections contextualised by my professional career
in high-performance settings in the National Rugby League (Australia),
Super League (United Kingdom), Scottish Rugby Union, Irish Rugby Union
and Australian Rugby Union.

Many aspects will reinforce commonly accepted methodologies while other
areas will question the theory and common practice of coaching. It is not
my intention to cloud the reader's thinking but to provide a realistic view. My
journey highlights emotional challenges that may deter the aspiring coach,
but ultimately the significance of choosing to be a coach will fall with you.

While writing this book, it became obvious that coaching style is forever
evolving as a result of experience and personal development. My experience
offers a diverse array of workplaces represented by cultural and social
challenges. Working in diverse environments has provided both positive
and negative aspects to my development. Experience holds the key to your
development. I hope that you accept this analogy as part of your journey.

My task is to identify, dissect and rationalise my learning that supports the
notion of experience as necessary to success. Shaped by many influences,
this learning provides a glimpse of reality, reward and the emotional
challenge of understanding your role as coach.

Section One discusses mentors as fundamental to establishing philosophical
views of coaching. Accepting support has many benefits including an
acknowledgement of the need to build your knowledge base to complement
learning.

It would be negligent not to reference those periods that challenged my
resolve because they were often catalysts to exploring the mechanics of

coaching. I learnt there is no magic wand to replace experience as the foundation to coaching. Loss and failure are fundamental to shaping the character of the coach.

I will discuss these periods of my development to highlight the psychology of coaching and how knowing your environment provides depth and context to your theory. As a young coach, these periods made me aware of the demands of coaching, but my ability to adapt was as critical in my development.

Section Two discusses the challenge of coaching the best athletes and it identifies the diverse demands on elite coaches. Working with the elite is the pinnacle of coaching, and demanding innovation while remaining contemporary is the greatest challenge. I will also discuss the idiosyncrasies of developing leaders and the importance of leadership groups in team sport. Understanding the necessity and role of senior leaders inside team development is a critical factor to the coach-athlete dynamic. Chapter 5 provides an up close and personal view of success and how my learning from that period set the foundation to the philosophical views and principles of the coaching I am presenting.

Success is discussed as being determined by experience, knowledge and skill; it is where coach philosophy may change as a consequence of events. My lessons from this period were a wake-up call to the use of data management. Managing the coach environment and succession planning is central to achieving success.

Section Three speaks of the surrounding coaching environment. Discussion targets the issues of conflict that occur as a result of the dynamics of ineffective operations. Examples clearly depict communication as central to effective teams.

I have presented loyalty and respect as paramount for success, while conflict between philosophy and integrity leads to disharmony. Importantly, the organisation's character is discussed as significant in determining a coach's tenure.

Professionalism is presented as a contradiction where perception of success, high performance and integrity collide. Defining professionalism is problematic on many levels, while working in environments that have unclear operational boundaries often results in chaos.

Section Four discusses change, review and high performance as critical elements of the business. My discussion focuses on the implications of change and its consequence. Change is defined as a mechanism to keep the environment fluid and contemporary.

High performance demands excellence. I discuss excellence and elite performance as relevant to all aspects of the organisation if success is to be achieved. Appropriately qualified staff, resourcing and planning are discussed as foundational elements of high-performance settings.

I have found coaching is broadly shaped by character, values and standards. My journey is one of self-realisation and acknowledging my frailty of character, which often challenged my worthiness as a coach. Personally, the social psychology of coaching suggests the enormity of mastering the art of coaching. For me, the real skill of coaching lies within the appreciation of learning, self-development and being committed to enabling others.

# ACKNOWLEDGMENTS

Writing this book has been challenging in many ways and much harder than I'd expected, while the process has been therapeutic and rewarding. Much of the work has been inspired by close friends and professional colleagues while my wife, Maree, and son, Brent, have shown patience throughout the process. Thank you.

Chris Anderson, Peter Ryan, Rod Kafer, Ray Herring, Tawera Nikau, Matt Rodwell, Scott Sattler, Kevin Campion, Matt Geyer, Gary Gold, Mick Byrne, Marcel Brache, Onehunga Mata'uiau, Cameron Blades and Matt Williams all provided valuable contributions and I am grateful for their wisdom. Thank you all.

I'd like to specially mention those who provided commentary while drafting the manuscript, in particular Sebastian Delport and Bob Hunter for your insights. Thanks also to the publishing team at Tellwell Talent.

Finally, thank you to my mentors who provided the catalyst for this book.

# PRAISE FOR THIS BOOK

"Possibly the best coaching book I've read since Bill Walsh's The Score Takes Care of Itself."

- Gary Gold (Head Coach, USA Rugby)

"A Coach's Journey provides a great resource of highly useful and practical teachings and insights into the life and journey of a great coach. I encourage you to take the time to enjoy, digest and apply them."

- Bob Hunter (Chief Executive Officer, Western Australian Rugby Union)

"This coaching manifesto is a must read, a resource ledger, a vital piece of equipment for aspiring and professional coaches and high-performance administrators while serving as a reference point to reflect on."

- Darren Soppa (Retired Police Inspector)

# SECTION ONE

# Coaching Influences — Actions and behaviours that have guided my development as a coach

*"The coach must get the best out of every player and show him how to work for the team to enable other players; he needs to know what makes each player tick. Senior players set the platform for the rest of the team: some by example and some by talking.*

*You must level the conversation to 'all things footy' to challenge the players during preparation and build a game plan so the player has an opportunity to impose their skill on their position and so things are recognizable to them. Once this relationship is established you can impose your personality.*

*Club culture is vital to winning, and being able to play your best under pressure is what makes champions. Dealing with pressure is a learnt skill where the more you place yourself under pressure the better you handle it as a team and as an individual. Clubs with good culture know how to win."*

- Chris Anderson (former Australian Kangaroos Rugby League World Cup winning head coach; National Rugby League premiership winning coach; Canterbury Bulldogs and Melbourne Storm Premiership winning coach; Member Halifax, UK Hall of Fame)

Having worked with Chris at both the national and club level, building the "right environment" is essential for player development. He recognises coach development, communication and senior players as significant to understanding culture.

Chris suggests the need for the coach to understand the immediate environment as a precursor for team performance; but it is also significant for your own development as a coach. In addition, recognise that support is critical for your maturation as a coach. Understanding these key elements of coaching will build winning teams. These critical areas of your development are never-ending and will remain a constant companion throughout your coaching journey.

The following chapters provide a summary of my early development. They discuss my mentors as well as some moments and decisions that led to pursuing coaching as a career. At a personal level, I have referred to those people who influenced my intrigue for coaching and guided me in my formative years. These accounts provide a logical framework for my interpretation of coaching and isolate several experiences that supported my transition from amateur to professional coach.

My discussion reveals an immaturity as I stuck to early learnings, some of which remained throughout my journey. Early senior appointments and new coaching experiences provided a platform to challenge my knowledge. Early traits are evident in my coaching today, while I consider continuous improvement as central to my growth.

Other early learning reveals many discerning behaviours, feelings and actions toward the foundation of coaching. There were periods of arrogance and immaturity that, naturally, hindered my development. The significance of having a mentor became obvious when I was trying to identify what defined me as a coach.

The benefit of relating to who you are as a person becomes obvious, but an understanding of the psychology of coaching was largely missing during my early appointments. Given experience, I realised that coaching is as much about being a mentor as it is about being a therapist of sorts.

So, how did I end up coaching? What precursors led to an interest around leadership and mentoring? Who influenced and supported my career path? Why coaching?

This section isolates early influences into the how and why of my coaching career.

# CHAPTER 1

# Shaping Your Role as Coach

To realise my ability and growth as a coach it was critical to have guidance from people who were prepared to share their knowledge and experience. Fortunately, many people have supported and continue to challenge my potential. This is a vital ingredient to ensuring your development remains fluid and continuous.

I was fortunate in some respects to graduate through the ranks (not by design) before finding my way into high-performance environments. After many years, the appreciation of learning remains one of my focuses, while the intrigue of new appointments and teaching continues to challenge my understanding of my role as a coach.

Today, I can take stock of these questions and consider those influences in my career by using examples of moments and challenges in my journey to decipher critical lessons that have contributed to my development as a professional coach.

Many of my references in the following accounts have subtle messages, while others have strongly influenced my coaching methods. Of great significance is the player–coach relationship from my youth and how that has shaped my behaviour in leadership, mentoring and coaching situations. Understanding the athlete will vary depending on the existing or potential for that bond to form. Building the relationship between coach and athlete is an undertaking defined by the challenge and subtlety and complexity of coaching.

## Profile

I was born in a small Queensland country town called Springsure. It is a rural hub for primary industry and coal mining. The region thrived on sport and recreational pursuits and has produced champions across many sports.

Although I had a competitive rugby league playing career, I'd always had an interest in coaching, and at the age of seventeen I entered the junior coaching ranks. By twenty-five I was coaching in a semi-professional environment whilst still playing. My relationship with my early coaches was indicative of my (developing) personality. If there was an early indication that suggested coaching would be my chosen career, it was the sense of fulfilment I gained from sport.

Closer to home, my coaches thrived on discipline and in some respects stifled my learning and development, particularly those mentors who lived vicariously through others. Maybe their use of discipline contributed to our success but the manner in which they coached offers a sense of clarity to the link between hard work and realising success.

Sports dominated my youth and the necessary pathways and competitions aided my competitive edge. From an early age I felt compelled to compete. That undoubtedly influenced my attitudinal development in some small part. The strength of my resolve to manage confrontations that arise as a coach came from those early battles. I developed a resolve that would be tested as a professional coach when I needed to embrace loss and failure as a part of learning.

## Early Coaches

A good starting point is to discuss my early coaches who provided many lessons in life and coaching that have lasted throughout my career. Their lessons played a significant part in my early development. They not only created a learning platform for athletic and skill development, but also nurtured my personality, which characterises my philosophy of coaching today. Personally, I feel we overlook the influence coaching has on our players' lives, personal growth and their role in society. Many past players that I have coached often discuss lessons learnt in their youth as providing direction in their lives today. As a coach, these stories resonate with me as to the part we play in their lives.

Many early styles of coaching have left their impression on me. They were all different but significant to my early development. The following accounts define my coaches' styles in a manner that was conducive to my early learning. These are my accounts, and they are offered with care and admiration for their support of my development.

- The Leader

I played for the Emerald Tigers in the Central Highlands for my junior rugby, which was a fantastic lesson on life's journey. As a player, I did not realise the lessons that were being handed out by coaches of that era or understand how those lessons would guide me through tough times as a coach and affect my general behaviour.

One coach who influenced me greatly was Brian O'Callaghan, also known as "Colonel." I have vivid memories of Brian coming to training in his army clobber and the immediate attention he commanded from us, built from the respect he had created between the players, parents and supporters. Brian espoused strong values reflecting discipline and commitment built from a platform of hard work, while care and respect for one another underpinned our training environment. The characteristics of that environment reflect the priorities in my coaching today.

Looking back through those early lessons, Brian enabled problem-solving and ownership of actions that in some ways conflicted with his strong leadership style and high expectations of our performances. Unbeknown to us at this stage of our development, Brian offered many life lessons whereby respect for work and reward for performance were interwoven in our training and playing environments. Those learnt skills continue to underpin my personal and career behaviours today. Of note, my coaching environment demands precision, learning and positive reinforcement.

- The Mate

One of my early senior coaches, Jack Hornery (Emerald Tigers, Central Highlands), was flamboyant and subtle in his coaching. He had years of playing experience and placed a strong focus on teambuilding and encouraging bonds within the group. He knew the game, but, more importantly, he could communicate his knowledge in simple but effective ways, acting more as a mate than as a coach.

Most of my tutelage from Jack came from his pre-match build-ups and chats over a beer after training while reviewing the match video — somewhat of an innovation for bush coaching in the early 1980s. His style highlighted the significance of teamwork. There was little science to his approach, and success was built on a common cause and camaraderie amongst the players. Successful in his own right, Jack's lasting message for me was built around mateship and building teams out of those bonds.

- The Respectful Coach

As an aspiring player, I was fortunate to be coached by Ian Thinee. Ian, a member of the Queensland Rugby League Hall of Fame, worked primarily on the theory of hard work, discipline and responsibility to the team. A soft-spoken man, Ian was rarely flustered, and he led with non-stop commitment as a player–coach. He gave 100% as a player and this approach flowed into his coaching and expectations of his players.

For me, his leadership style demanded a strong work ethic and "giving all" in every action. His methods were simple but reflected his character and sense of purpose to his players.

At a recent reunion, many of the plaudits went in the direction of Ian for his outstanding contribution to one of the oldest Rugby League clubs in Australia: the Fitzroy Sharks, Rockhampton. It was well-deserved recognition for his longstanding service as a player, coach and administrator. True to his nature, Ian was humble and respectful of his peers, recognising those players and committee members who had gone before him.

I have never forgotten Ian's humility and the respect he had for his players and the game itself.

- The Modern Coach

Alan Smith as head coach of Surfers Paradise Sharks, Gold Coast, brought innovative ideas to training that he learned as a professional rugby league player for teams including the North Sydney Bears and Canberra Raiders (NSWRL competition) and Queensland. He provided a learning environment that was varied, challenging and fun. I thoroughly enjoyed playing under Smithy with the bonus of also playing outside him as a player. His knowledge of the game was unquestioned and the respect that he gained from the players was obvious.

Alan was modern, and he challenged the way we thought about the game and how we prepared. He was the first coach that emphasised the necessity of quality of training and linked it to match performance.

- The Taskmaster

Ross Strudwick (former Queensland and Australian Rugby League player and head coach of Brisbane Valleys, Past Brothers and London Broncos) carried that education into his coaching. I learnt that you earn your selection through performance in the match. Reputations meant nothing when it came to weekly selections. Coming from regional Queensland, this was new to me as I struggled to provide consistency of performance while adapting to the weekly demands of Brisbane club rugby.

The physical and psychological challenges presented by Struddy shaped my early coaching style. His methods provided the basis for selection, where commitment is king. These standards governed my approach to coaching in the professional game where standards commensurate to elite performance are paramount.

- The Innovator

Phil Hortz (former Brisbane Past Brothers, Brisbane Rugby League player) was a very good coach who provided a glimpse of the principles I call "modern coaching." I initially met Phil when he was the Gold Coast State League representative coach. He later became my club coach in Beaudesert, Gold Coast. He was accessible and impressed upon me the importance of building relationships with the player. Phil's passion for the game was infectious, which made for some interesting coaching sessions, but there was always an educational slant to his methods that was designed to challenge and explore our limits.

Phil demonstrated a collaborative style of coaching and used well-planned sessions delivered through various methods, such as player–coach performance reviews and use of external facilitators inside the training environment. At the time, these methods were innovative and engaging.

Phil was a student of the game and his sessions reflected a learning environment that has influenced me greatly in how I approach my coaching. At that point in my career, I knew that coaching would be a major part of my life.

- The Introvert

Peter Inskip was soft spoken and very experienced in the game. I met him when he was head coach of the Gold Coast Queensland State League squad. "Skippy" was another coach who had competed at the highest levels of the modern game as a professional player (Canterbury Bankstown and North Sydney, NSWRL) and proficiently demonstrated the art of representative coaching.

Pete's coaching style was loosely planned, which was conducive to preparing a representative squad. This program relied heavily on senior player experience to guide team coaching principles and strategies. As a squad member, I felt that these methods were effective, efficient and appropriate.

His program gave players room to explore and navigate their way through the process, but with the same expectations and outcomes driving his goals — winning. His style created a comfortable setting that enabled collaborative learning whereby the coach acted as a facilitator who encouraged individual and team styles to develop.

- The Measured Coach

Geoff Naylor (former head coach Southern Suburbs Magpies, Brisbane Rugby League) was a coach I instantly respected. It was Geoff who introduced me to senior-grade coaching (while still playing). As with previous coaches, I became a student of Geoff's approach to the coaching environment. As the club's head coach, he managed his staff, program and players with apparent ease. Knowing now what is expected of the head coach I have greater appreciation of Geoff's influence to my development as a coach. My greatest observation and learning from Geoff's skill was his overarching management style. He was well-presented and prepared and conveyed a sense of calm that resonated with the playing group and staff.

## Lessons

As a player, I was exposed to very astute coaches that offered contrasting styles, attitudes and approaches to coaching. They were all effective in their own way and certainly shaped my coaching philosophy and approach.

I have found that coaching inevitably shapes how you develop as a person. Many of my influences and early experiences from previous coaches remain relevant today, while my personality dictates the behaviour that I feel fits the environment.

- Character

Observing and modelling your coaching on any one individual may result in confusion and uncertainty for the player. Understanding who you are is vital. Work within your own character and those needs of your environment. Ensure that nurturing and development remain fundamental to your action as a coach and that your athletes remain your central focus. Your character must lead the way to how you convey your teachings. Understand that the significance of who you are should play a major part in developing your coaching character.

I was fortunate that strong personalities shaped my youth, behaviour and actions, which inevitably became precursors to my development as a coach. Gradually, I managed to discover my own style of coaching, but only when I accepted who I was as a person and how effective that could be in my role as a coach.

The significance of developing your own style is paramount to identifying with your role as a coach and mentor. Understanding yourself will provide the platform for developing coaching methods and this knowledge in turn improves you.

- Style

As a young coach, I shaped my style through various associations and sources, but as my experience and knowledge grew, so did my confidence. This gradually led to a style that is forever fluid in process and application as my personality continues to be shaped.

My junior, senior and representative coaches all had their own methods. Some were authoritarian and direct, while others were astute and tactical and offered a guiding hand that crossed into players' personal lives.

All my coaches and mentors possessed qualities that in some way influenced my decision to pursue coaching. Making the jump from playing to coaching was not by design or through a supported pathway. I learnt "on the hop" that my decision to coach was initially prompted by others who saw competencies in me that suited coaching. I suggest that this would generally be the case for many who decide to pursue coaching in the first instance. Being exposed to a cross-section of coaching styles helped immensely in my formative years as a coach, and I often drew upon methods I observed in my early mentors.

Exposure to tactical coaching, with no disrespect to my mentors, was limited and came later in my career. Building tactics comes from experience and trial and error, while the relationship between tactics and strategy and their use will vary dependent on an opponent's weaknesses and your team's strengths. Managing this information in regard to preparation is a learnt skill and will again take experience to master its application.

- Knowing the Individual

Underpinning all my lessons has been my willingness to understand the individual and enable their skill and game sense development. Applied skills, rugby intellect and identifying key decision-makers provide a path for finding the appropriate tactics that fit your squad. From experience, imposing tactics your playing group without catering for the squad's tactical nous will lead to random success.

## Defining Self as a Coach

So, what defines you as a coach? This question has intrigued me for as long as I have understood the effects of poor communication in coaching. For me, the single most important facet of coaching is being an effective communicator so that your knowledge can be deciphered, managed and enacted by the players. I look for signs that signify information is being applied, which provides a sense of validation to the coaching environment.

To me, coaching is an outlet to sell my ideas on the game as much as it is an opportunity to lead and mentor. Even at an early stage of coaching I enjoyed sharing knowledge. How you communicate your knowledge is key.

As a junior coach, I knew I had to motivate, lead and also communicate game knowledge in a manner that the player could understand and use inside a game. For many years, I struggled to find the balance between the detail and transforming that information into effective performance. The key is to blend your information to a point at which the player's ability dictates the content. The effectiveness of your communication is ultimately measured by how well the training performance transfers to competition. Experience helps find that balance in some respects, but understanding your environment remains critical to enabling the communication between coach, player and, ultimately, the experience.

Through my early experiences and coaching influences, I am more informed on how to manage players and their environment. As a coach, I deliberately find those quiet players in the group who lack prominence to ensure they are being supported. That defines coaching for me. Coaching the few dominant and skilled characters is an easy route, while coaching those who sit back in the various layers inside the main playing group provides a greater sense of depth and challenge to your coaching. By-passing the "senior player" to chat openly to the less dominant player also demonstrates your style of acceptance for all in your coaching environment.

My decision to become a coach can best be understood by how I evolved as a person. As my character and confidence grew, so too did my respect for the knowledge I possessed, as players listened and acted on that information. Early on, the win–loss ratio had little bearing on my career development as a coach, as I was more attuned to the fact that I had knowledge I felt needed to be shared regardless of the outcome.

- Why Coach?

At twenty-five years of age, I fell into my initial semi-professional senior head coach role, and to this day, I have no idea why I accepted the position. Mostly, I did not want to let down those who had recommended and supported me for that role. The other side was an opportunity to test myself, which had always been part of my make-up.

Personally, working with people and enjoying the game presented itself as a potential platform from which to pursue professional coaching. My passion for the game also led to other questions around the task of coaching such as whether I was suitable (others thought so). At these times you question your own credibility, confidence and ability to lead, which for me provides the greatest challenge!

Had I not enjoyed the game in the first instance, coaching would have been a chore and certainly would not have been on the menu. I assume that many have fallen into coaching roles because they were influenced by their peers, as I had done previously as a junior coach. My challenge was setting about to test my knowledge and accept that I had something of value to offer.

The desire to self-educate and pass on that information to others was always on my mind, as reflected in my early entry to coaching. In no way did I feel I was an authority on the game, but I felt I had information that was worth sharing.

I was always a student of sport, so learning and becoming a coach was part of that stepped education. Coaching provides a means to validate your ability to manage, transfer knowledge and educate. My advice is that if you do not have those ingredients, coupled with a willingness to take risks, do not coach. This is certainly the case at a professional level, where trying something new can be a challenge and actually demands innovation and risk.

## Your Role as the Coach

My desire to acquire knowledge has provided the "teach, correct and remediate" approach to coaching. My early coaches had this common link while striving for continuous improvement from their players. I am no different in that respect.

To gain any insight into the playing group, coaching must be considered teaching. Teaching demands that you develop your students while trying to make the experience pleasurable. You need to enjoy the coaching experience to truly reach your goals or those of your players, and this applies to any level of coaching. Lose the enjoyment of coaching and you challenge your ability to teach or communicate effectively.

My role as a coach is underlined by how to improve personally, but it also considers how I improve those in my charge. This is the single most important point of defining my role as coach. The term "correction" is often shunned in today's world of political correctness and I can testify from experience that finding the balance between constructive feedback and how players interpret that feedback is a challenge. Being aware of the tone, manner and content of your exchanges, and how that may be interpreted by the athlete is a constant challenge particularly when coaching youth. Creating a learning environment with development in mind is surely our priority as coaches. Having the means to enable a suitable method of correction at the forefront of your coaching is key to the development of your players.

Former Brisbane Broncos NRL Premiership winner Kevin Campion said of his mentor and highly acclaimed professional coach Wayne Bennett: *"The head coach took an interest not only in your football but also in your home life. He knew when you were having trouble at home by the way you were performing. He really cared and the more he cared the more I wanted to do my best. When you have 17 players wanting to play for their coach it's a team that's very hard to beat."*

# CHAPTER 2

# Learning on the Run

Even as an aspiring coach, I had a semblance of knowledge of what to do, but it takes many years of hard work and education to be truly defined as a coach who can balance the organisation and players' goals to be on the winners' podium. If we were honest as coaches, we would acknowledge periods of uncertainty or times when we lacked clarity and were buried in confusion over our role.

From a learning perspective, my early appointments as a coach were critical to my development. That realisation did not occur at the time, but it is an admission I make upon reflection. There was no one to highlight the potential pitfalls of these appointments — just dive in and do your best. For most, that was the accepted norm during this period.

Early appointments tested how much I really wanted to be a coach. What I didn't understand at the time was that my apprenticeship (early appointments) was necessary if I was to progress to professional appointments at the highest level of sport, which I was fortunate to experience.

I was young, but I had a sense of maturity; I considered and understood, to a point, that these decisions would in some way influence my future. Some of those decisions resulted in failure, when risk outweighed the reward. However, in the scheme of the journey, it was an invaluable learning platform. The tough times I navigated provided an opportunity to develop the leadership, management and planning skills that are so important in my coaching.

Two head coach roles during this early period of my development laid the foundation for my coaching. Although I was impatient, I am thankful that I understood the need to accept these roles as a learning phase in my development. Like all young, aspiring coaches, I was on the "fast train" but with a sense of direction driven by my own thirst for knowledge.

These opportunities also provided an avenue to explore my own coaching principles, particularly in preparation, teaching and developing the squad. Each game I coached was an opportunity to challenge my communication, leadership skills and tactical nous.

**Setting – Scene 1**

At twenty-five years old, I was appointed third-grade head coach at Southern Suburbs in the Brisbane Rugby League (1988). I was also a club selector and a graded player, all of which amounted to a seven-days-a-week commitment. This was an era when coaches, players and staff held full-time jobs, so I was certainly time-poor, but I was driven to learn as much as I could.

Souths' first-grade head coach was Geoff Naylor (former Queensland representative; Balmain Sydney, NSWRL player), a very articulate, measured and dedicated coach. Geoff's coaching was modern, technical and astute. Tactically, he was well prepared and thoroughly considered from both the opposition viewpoint and our team's game plan. He was a very deliberate coach, as demonstrated by his consistency in squad selection and his creation of a challenging learning environment. Players and staff had great respect for him as a person and mentor.

Although Geoff was obliging in his support, he required his coaches (and players) to own their responsibilities, which in a way fast-tracked my learning and tested both my commitment and dedication to coaching. During my time at Souths, Geoff guided the team to the minor premiership (1988), but, unfortunately, we were bundled out in straight sets and lost the major and preliminary finals.

It was fortunate for me that there were many talented and experienced players on the squad who all became silent mentors (e.g., Bob Kellaway, Brad Tessmann, Mark Meskell, Bruce Harry, Richo Hill and Keith Gee). This was invaluable and allowed me to observe senior player and coach relations.

## Being the Rookie Coach

Coaching the third-grade side had its own challenges, none greater than being young and aspiring. I tested my methods against some very hardened players, but it was crucial in my coaching career because I learnt to deal with egos and "out of form" graded players. As a result, I developed negotiation, arbitration and mediation skills.

The mix of squad members meant I had to ensure my sessions were structured to challenge. I worked with young, aspiring players whose expectations often outweighed their abilities — an example of the many (emotional) juggling acts you confront as a lower-grade coach.

Remembering that this was my initial senior-grade appointment and having minimal experience to draw upon, I recall how quickly my excitement turned to panic once I realised the task ahead. I was soon to realise the complexities of the role, which often left me struggling for answers — another lesson whereby you find the solution by counsel or your own device.

My lack of practical experience as a coach created many challenges. I could say I had a very clear vision of how training should go and how our matches should be played, but that would be untrue. That was never going to be the case — it is hard enough in a professional environment with many resources, let alone coaching a squad full of players with misgivings, misled aspirations and dented egos. That was one of the real challenges for a lower-grade coach, but it was invaluable as a rookie coach at so many levels. Communicating with experienced players would be tested many times during my professional career.

Being an apprentice, I approached each situation with trepidation and regularly sought advice from the club's senior coaches and players. As the season unfolded, I found innovative methods of keeping the players motivated, which was critical as a lower-grade coach. Adaptability was my saviour. On the plus side, there were young players who wanted to achieve, and I found the greatest rewards in that area.

## Lessons

Maybe I have overplayed this in my coaching but knowing the character and "group-think" of the squad ensures your program meets their needs. Accordingly, individual mentoring sits high on my list of priorities, while unit and team coaching provides the essential rudiments for collective implementation of strategies.

Even during this early phase, I gravitated to working at an individual level while other key facets of my development were to take shape. Individual coaching enables a far more complete approach to your work and transference of theory and practice. Managing this process is time consuming but beneficial as a method for imparting knowledge and learning.

- Diversity

As a coach, you must realise that the diversity of personalities is fundamental to the playing group. It is as important as being adaptable. A lesson to all lower-grade coaches is to be prepared for last-minute challenges and the ever-changing range of characters who will enter your squad during any given season. Preparation is paramount and will actually assist when those last-minute changes are forced upon you. So, catering for compromise to achieve an acceptable performance is reliant on how effective your contingency planning is.

Character, game maturity and varying skill sets thrown together in a team provide many challenges as you seek buy-in from your players. In many ways, coaching at this level is more challenging than at first grade. It may lack the intensity and the strategy of top-flight competition, but as far as man management is concerned, it is vital.

This mix of youth and senior players creates challenges on and off the field. Stepping my way through the diversity of characters was certainly a test of my patience and ability to manage players and stay true to my coaching philosophy. As coach you need to manage your coaching principles in a manner that is relevant to your environment. This does not mean that your values as a person change, nor does it mean the foundations of your coaching philosophy should change. They should merely function as a subset of your environment.

Training sessions at this level need to have plenty of variety but at the same time meet the demands of the ensuing match. The sessions during my tenure always included a range of skill rehearsal, game scenario practice and a semblance of a match plan that was a product of what we could deliver considering the ever-changing squad and disruption to preparation.

## Challenges

Accept that change is ever-present in your coaching week. Your challenge is to hold true to your coaching principles and embrace the early struggles when you accept your initial appointment as a lower-grade or assistant coach. You must become adaptable and accept these struggles as an opportunity to test the range of your skills as a coach.

Being true to your methods is a challenge, as constant changes to your squad mean you must alter your program. Player movement is a constant threat, as are injuries and selection changes. Again, these challenges test your resolve and ability to adjust on the run, but they also enable you to develop squad management and coordination skills.

There are very few coaching roles in which every player buys-in to your philosophy in the first instance, let alone dealing with constant disruption (e.g., squad changes). While this is happening, your job is to maintain your philosophy and see this aspect as part of the journey! Finding the balance between the players' skill, game sense and your principles will remain a constant companion during your coaching career. Failure to recognise these potential challenges will result in a constant battle with the player in your role as a mentor while your philosophy becomes challenged by uncertainty.

The greatest challenge for a young, aspiring coach is to find the right appointment. There was no "development plan" I could refer to when I was coming through the system because so much of what we did was by accident. Today we have a pathway system for our coaches with experienced mentors to tutor them. My advice is to consider any potential appointment in the context of what you want to gain out of the role. If an appointment is considered as part of your career journey to be a professional coach, my advice is to seek counsel.

- Balancing Goals

Coaching is ever-changing. One process, system or approach will not fit all. As a lower-grade coach, my first realisation was that the coaching environment is dynamic and cluttered with egos and personalities which require shared attention. This point is actually relevant to all levels of coaching. Aspirations, goals and expectations will, at some point, be conflicted — your job is to provide a sense of reality where the individual, team and organisation are working within some form of "commonality."

While the organisation (club) provides a set of standards and goals, for the coach, developing the individual underpins team success. Being able to acknowledge the player's status as the focus must be a priority within your role as a coach. At times this may challenge the team's goals. Integrating individual and team aspirations offers collective responsibilities that are very important to the athlete's development. What I thought was "coaching" was being challenged. To be fluid in thinking and adaptable in approach are key.

## Player Centred

Setting out to understand your environment is a crucial step to realising the team's goals and fundamental to appreciating the demands of both player and squad.

Critical to my coaching is defining the considerations that exist between the individual, team and organisation goals. What has worked for me is considering the individual as the key — both from understanding the person and supporting that player to realise his goals.

A player-centred approach allows the individual to challenge their role, provide answers and then discuss how their decisions fit within the team. This statement does not lessen your responsibility as coach but merely underlines the need to support the individual. We all have differing aspirations even within a team context. Guiding, rather than telling, and encouraging a collaborative approach between coach and squad is key to effective buy-in and building a sense of ownership.

The diagram below illustrates the challenge of finding an efficient means of working with the individual while considering the many demands! Each player deserves time, while planning provides the means to managing your time and program around the athlete, team and overarching goals.

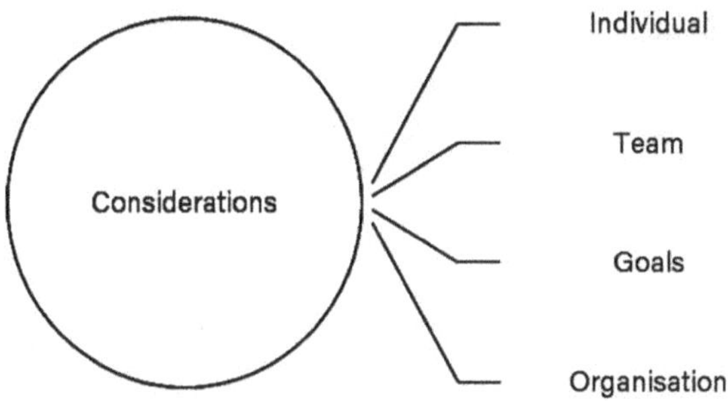


- Coaching Focus

My time as a lower-grade coach revealed the value of one-to-one coaching, and I certainly became more attuned to the importance of the following constructs:

- Game-oriented learning is a priority to test game situations, applied position and skill
- Emphasis can be on skill acquisition and remedial practices as key to the context of the game and the development of the player
- Focus can readily shift from skill-based learning to game-related execution and applied movements
- Provide a platform of game-based practice where transference of position-specific requirements can be observed and corrected
- Create opportunities to analyse athlete application and applied learning in game-specific moments
- Enable a controlled environment where 360-degree feedback can be provided between player and coach.

These key points should be adjusted to age, maturity and game knowledge in terms of knowledge and playing experience. The basis for skill and position learning is an obvious rehearsal element while game-related practice affords more opportunities to assess and correct applied techniques.

## Setting - Scene 2

If I thought my initial semi-professional coaching appointment was a difficult initiation, my next appointment at Milton Keynes (BARLA, England) offered up a new set of challenges.

As a player in this era (1988-89), you could go to the UK and play their season without interfering with your competition in Australia. That has since changed as both seasons now run concurrently.

Adjusting quickly to varying training circumstances (including the weather) became a skill, but what surprised me was the varying degree of commitment. This was a huge shock and one of the major challenges during this season, but it also provided an invaluable learning platform.

The challenge of coaching amateur players was a tough assignment but again provided many lessons. Not least of these was finding new methods to keep players motivated. Upon reflection, the season at Milton Keynes was another crucial step in my development as a coach, although at the time I did not realise just how important it was.

Milton Keynes was a great adventure, but, more importantly, it provided flagposts to my development as a coach and took my apprenticeship to another level.

## Lessons

My greatest lesson was to acknowledge that attitude and personality will ultimately affect performance. That is no real surprise. Attitude can relate to a host of individual or team disciplines such as commitment to training, willingness to accept criticism or being empathic to others and their challenges.

As with attitude, personality can relate to individual or team-based traits necessary for performance. Group approaches in a learning environment also have obvious merit, while understanding personality may create other forms of learning conducive to consistent, clinical or disciplined performances. These are all important considerations to team planning.

With that knowledge, constructing a plan for success should be easy. Surely, the trick for success is to assemble a squad that reflects like-minded people who have a similar attitude for success, right? That thinking was another moment of immaturity, as I would learn in future years.

## Professional Development

During this period, I developed my thirst for knowledge outside the normal coaching spheres. I had undertaken university studies as I tried to understand the link between culture, learning and behaviour as possible factors in delivering consistent performance.

Sourcing material from different disciplines, including management, psychology and organisational behaviour, gave me a broader insight into the coaching environment. The day you tire of learning is the day to retire as a coach. Your goal should be to create an environment of continuous development for yourself and for players.

If you continue to challenge your knowledge and method of coaching, the players invariably benefit. Seeking other sources of learning will assist you to provide a deeper understanding of your role as a leader, coach and mentor.

Keeping my coaching environment unique meant being adaptable to each training session that challenged my knowledge and style. Coaching in an amateur environment drove me to self-education, as the complexities of coaching became more apparent and the need to broaden my coaching scope was required.

Needing to know how to better manage players with varying levels of commitment and to challenge the players with a greater depth of knowledge can only benefit your coaching.

- Journal

Recording your training sessions enables you to track the progress of your players, programs and performance; this is crucial for the team's development. Tracking is a learnt skill and forming the habit in the first instance is essential. The process does not have to be all-consuming, but finding what areas fit your coaching style can be challenging. Refining the process will come only as a product of a habit.

Your journal notes will highlight critical details that have influenced session plans, season programs and long-term development strategies for the team. Entries can be as detailed as you need — the key is the purpose.

For example, I divided various disciplines such as well-being, athletic and game development, as well as session critiquing that included individual correction notes. These areas are important at the professional and amateur level. Recording may be less detailed at lower levels, but the purpose of your tracking should be to monitor your training, evaluate the progress of the season plan and measure how the sessions track in the performance of each player.

Today, much of our knowledge is data-supported, which allows progress to be tracked with software that enables the coach to view sessions immediately while an analyst edits upon request for correction purposes. Sessions are populated with all sorts of devices including drones that provide a "bird's-eye" view of training performance. This is instant journal support for player and coach!

- Variety in Learning

Coaching, aside from its primary purpose of teaching, should be fun and exciting. This is necessary to keep your role challenging, invigorating and rewarding. You can become too caught up in the detail and miss the essence of the game, as I learnt through experience.

The real ability is to decipher the many hours of video, analyse statistics and determine how they can influence a winning performance. Doing more is not always the answer. The detail (analysis and data) must remain in a form that holds meaning for the player's development.

As coach, you must teach and manage the delivery and content while correcting in a manner that provides meaning and context to the individual, their goals and outcomes. Too often we lose sight of our roles, failing to construct our work so that it is about teaching the player how to improve an applied skill that will ultimately develop their game. Coaching in the moment is prevalent to player, action and performance outcome. This means being able to coach unscripted — a disciplined skill.

Continually challenging and refining how you construct your sessions is to ensure simplicity. Energy to meet a desired outcome (e.g., completing an attacking sequence without fault, where applied skill and execution operated with precision and control) is fundamental to providing inspiration and continuous improvement for the players. Injecting variation to lighten work volume and provide fun is a must at all levels of coaching but particularly at the amateur level. The material you provide should be steered toward learning and contextualised by athlete ability and maturity.

The coaching environment by default describes our roles as mentors and leaders in developing the players' learning and execution. Our goal is to maximise the athletes' talent through learning and education. Developing the individual to realise their potential should be a primary focus!

**Postscript by Peter Ryan** (defence coach Queensland Reds; former State of Origin Queensland representative; ACT Brumbies Super Rugby title winner and Brisbane Bronco NRL premiership winner; former assistant coach NRL Cowboys and Broncos)

*"Small gains make big changes."*

*As a coach I advise aspiring coaches that learning is built on self-education and patience, trial and error and experience. The more experience I gained, the more able I was to analyse and provide expertise. From a learning perspective I could say that my time as a professional player provided the necessary tools to be a coach, but that would be a stretch. Being fortunate to have played at the highest levels of competition has taught me discipline and an ability to relate to the mechanics and skill of the game — all necessary elements to be a coach. However, coaching is its own discipline and must be learnt.*

*Never underestimate your early mentors. In my case, my dad, Gerry Ryan, and my friend, Danny O'Brien (former Golden Gloves), were critical for my early coaching career. They taught me the technical aspects, game disciplines and "street smarts" such as: "protect myself; be proactive and win the punch (get in first)." I use these simple but effective analogies as essential in my coaching method — albeit in a scientific sense today. As a mentor, Wayne Bennett's "sink or swim" approach allowed me to find my own way, while my professional days as a player were an invaluable resource to draw upon.*

*Prior to accepting my first professional coaching appointment, the only experience I had was limited to working as a development officer at the Broncos and a senior player at the ACT Brumbies where I would provide support for defence sessions.*

*When I arrived at the Broncos as a professional coach (2006), it's no wonder I felt trepidation, pressure and the weight of expectation to succeed — a feeling no different from debuting as a player for the Broncos. I was overwhelmed to a point but turned up and went to work with what I knew would get the desired result.*

*"Learning on the run" was an understatement dotted by many obstacles as I was thrown into the deep end of professional coaching. An early reminder to the enormity of the task: I recall asking Wayne Bennett (Broncos head coach) what we were going to do with a certain player as his defence was not at NRL level. Wayne's response was 'You are the defence coach, what are you going to do with him?' Using my own "sense" of experience, I developed a program that saw the player complete 500+ tackles during his preseason before improvement was realised. I'm sure Wayne had my best interests at heart, but certainly this was a test.*

*This wasn't an ideal manner to be introduced to pro coaching as sole owner of the player's remedial program, but I found my way. From a technical perspective I learnt to build a program based on volume and education to initiate change, a process I have adapted over many years for corrective practices I use today that are uniquely mine.*

*Finally, and importantly, my approach to coaching reflects my values and standards in life: "work hard, demand effort on effort and an attitude of not letting your mate down." These traits evolved from my early mentors who shaped my role as coach.*

# Section Two

# Elite Coaching — Our best, our leaders and success

*"It is rare for successful teams to not have a symbiotic relationship between the head coach and senior players (leaders) within the team. Whilst there have been examples when this has occurred, the ACT Brumbies (Super Rugby franchise) in 2004 is a good example that demonstrates sustained success is rarely possible. Part of the head coach's core leadership responsibility is to build a relationship of trust with the senior players so in times of stress and conflict players are empowered to challenge the coach in order to develop team accountability and, ultimately, get results. Rod Macqueen AM (former Wallabies, NSW Waratahs, ACT Brumbies and Rebels head coach) was the best I have seen at understanding this dynamic of player empowerment."*

- Rod Kafer (former head coach Saracens Rugby; former Wallaby, World Cup representative; Super Rugby and Heineken Cup title winner, Leicester Tigers, UK)

The following chapters deal with the underlying and contrasting themes of elite coaching that suggest the boundary between success and failure rides on talent and leadership.

Drawing on experiences of a premiership, international fixtures and World Cups, I debate the essence of professionalism as a perception, whereby coaching the elite presents the same issues as coaching in an amateur setting.

This section presents leadership as critical to my coaching, in which succession plans and curriculum-based learning is geared toward those selected athletes that display "team first" attributes.

The case for leadership development is presented using examples that highlight the differing styles and qualities of the individuals who fit leadership roles.

Critically, in this discussion I provide experiences that contain characteristics of success dominated by a holistic operational approach, managed by high-achieving staff and the best athletes.

Significantly, compromise is deleted from the organisation's culture while challenging the boundaries of excellence is an accepted method for improving business focus. Constantly challenging your business, its process, system and staff underpin a culture of excellence, while success is the reward.

# Chapter 3

# Coaching at the Elite Level

The elite athlete sets exceptional standards and the desire to succeed consumes their being as they strive to be the best.

Coaching has certainly provided me with unique insight into the inner world of the elite athlete and their outer environment. There are obvious and not so obvious signs of what separates the elite from the rest. Common threads among the best are control, a standard that governs behaviour, resolve and dedication. The "one percenters" we speak about so often in coaching are readily seen in their approach, while their competitiveness amongst their peers is obvious. While their preparation is meticulous, the determination and will to seek perfection drives them to be the best.

So often I have watched careers fail not because of lack of talent, but because of an individual's lack of drive to succeed. Those who succeed consider failure as unacceptable, and achieving their dream rules their daily intent. Fortunately, I have witnessed and coached athletes who have defined their own greatness while a few sit at the "excellence" level of their sport. Those few provide a distinction that defines the elite athlete.

In this account, I provide some observations drawn from my time spent with the Australian National Rugby League squad (1998-2000). I discuss the environment of both the players and the coaches to demonstrate the dynamic that exists when coaching the elite. This account also provides a brief snapshot of that period's changing attitudes toward professionalism and the impact on the national squad.

**Setting the Scene**

Rugby League during the mid-1990s was going through dramatic change as pay TV had arrived with a massive injection of funds enabling development of the professional game. Clubs improved their operational structures, facilities and coaching models to meet the demands of this new era.

This period ushered in a greater involvement of player unions and agents, which in some ways forced much of the modernisation of the game. At a governance level, change was inevitable although met with some reluctance. The model at the time was somewhat outdated in how the game was perceived at the international level.

**Background**

The Australian Rugby League (ARL) managed the State of Origin and national programs, which saw international test matches arguably become secondary to the national competition and State of Origin series.

During my involvement with the national squad, I observed an obvious gap between the NRL clubs and the governing body's understanding of professionalism. Pay TV had already made a mark as clubs went about professionalising their systems. Conversely, much had remained unchanged in the national squad's preparations, including those systems such as resourcing and appropriate staff models.

My appointment as assistant coach resulted from an informal chat with the national coach. There was no formal application process, no interview or job description to speak of and hired help was at the head coach's discretion. His discretionary power was used to discuss my interest in the national role, which, of course, was met with a resounding "Yes!" We then went straight into mapping out a program.

In contrast, specialist coaching positions had existed at NRL clubs for many years, but this concept was still some time away for the national team. With respect, the ARL was out of touch with the modern game, leaving the national squad under-resourced! The support today for the national team is a far cry from this period, which reflects the modernisation of the international game.

The following references highlight a path toward the 2000 World Cup, mapped out over several years, and include samples of events that I feel provide context to coaching elite players.

## Team Dynamics

The 1999 Anzac Test formed part of the selection platform for the World Cup, which was some eighteen months away. The Test against New Zealand was dotted with classy moments by Australian players, which would present selection challenges in finalising the World Cup squad.

As a coaching staff, we had entered the match to win, but our secondary task was to observe the dynamic between the players, particularly the more experienced group: how they worked from within and how the squad responded to instruction from their captain and senior players.

Dealing with high-performing athletes can be perceived as simple as far as strategy and systems are concerned. Generally, this is the case, but managing elite players challenges your experience, knowledge and tactical nous, while athletic prowess and skill creates its own unique responsibilities of adapting and integrating best talent with team strategy in mind (i.e., position changes, interchange options).

The coaching environment at the elite level can be confrontational as the athletes search for their best performance, reward and recognition. The challenge is managing differing personalities and egos to ensure the team functions with balance. There are occasions when balance is challenged, and the team suffers.

This is where an individual may perceive their contribution to be more important than others'; there are times when team accolades are compromised at the expense of a stand-out moment initiated by a creative individual action or where the team wears the coach's rant due to a poor individual decision at the expense of team play. These are uneasy situations, but the opportunity to work with elite athletes in moments of brilliance is far greater reward then the odd occasion of imbalance of ego and attitude.

The following year, several changes were made to the squad to cater for retirement and player availability. The Anzac Test in 2000 was a fizzer, with the Kangaroos thrashing the Kiwis 52–nil. The bulk of this team would later form the backbone of the 2000 World Cup squad.

## Building a Performance Profile

The one-off matches against Papua New Guinea and New Zealand Residents along with the Anzac Test performances of 1999 and 2000 provided the platform for World Cup selection. Obviously, NRL club form and the State of Origin program also played a major part in squad selection. Each week we would profile our top players to build a depth chart, evaluate performance and provide regular feedback to those players under national consideration. Match evaluations took various forms but largely appeared as a statement of account against key position requirements.

This process requires a complete understanding between coach and athlete of how to set targets and their use within the athlete's capacity. Targets allow the individual to set position standards that require both an applied skill level and the ability to perform in game pressure.

Interpreting performance requires the coach and athlete to be on the same page. Defined performance standards and how those standards are achieved are to be measured. The "how, what and when" play a significant part at this stage in determining acceptable performance standards.

Reset (see below) refers to the resetting of targets once assessment is aligned between athlete and coach. Critically at this stage, corrected areas are rehearsed as part of the individual and team preparation prior to the next fixture. This cycle relies on an educated athlete who has the ability to reflect, deconstruct and constructively reset performance-based targets.

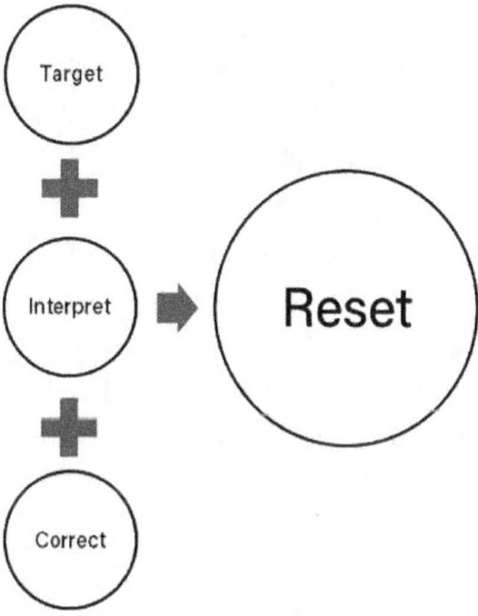


Indirectly we were building a performance log where consistency provides the key criterion for selection. Their positions were detailed to a point at which their primary role was continually measured against positional functions that would govern their roles in tournament. This material became a base level against which to measure their World Cup performances.

# Coaching Structure

Our model of coaching at the national level was very basic, largely due to the lack of resourcing for our program. As I mentioned, I felt that the governing body had been left behind in professionalising the national squad program.

With only Head Coach Chris Anderson and I managing the preparation, we frantically organised pre-tour content and analysis to ensure that the coaching program and player detail would be completed. The analysis work on our players and our World Cup opponents was predominantly completed before we left Australia.

To offset the lack of coaching support, our roles were simplified to alleviate the pressure of being too complex or detailed. Chris managed the overarching strategy while I supported his analogies with the appropriate analysis, player detail and opposition commentary. Individual analysis was a major component of our preparation, supported by extensive detail on positional evaluations and goal setting for the individual.

The senior player group also played a significant part in selection, game preparation and match planning while Chris and I filled the gaps. Obviously, our support staff were critical to the team's preparation and success.

## Selection

The squad largely picked itself after two years of profiling players' performances. However, there were still positional challenges, none more so than selecting our game managers. The intelligence required to manage a game at this level was fundamental to executing our systems.

These were hotly contested positions in a world-class squad. Club combinations and State of Origin performance was naturally a significant component of the selection process.

As a case in point, Melbourne Storm half, Brett Kimmorley, won selection over the more fancied NSW Origin half, Andrew Johns. Both were world-class athletes, but in this case team make-up would see Johns play out of position due to Kimmorley's selection at half-back. This was one of several difficult selections.

Both players possessed fantastic all-round skills with excellent kicking games. They were comfortable managing either side of the attacking shape and both were gifted leaders. It seems incredible but our squad was so talented that we were able to move players in positions to accommodate game strategy. This also provided validation of our pre-tournament selection policy of position skill, athletic durability and game sense as a criterion.

## Leadership

These elite players gave us many examples of leadership and its practical application. One standout moment was the application of tactical prowess and skill against world-class competitors that greatly influenced the outcome of the World Cup final playing New Zealand.

Chris and Captain Brad Fittler laid strategies for the second half. It wasn't unusual for the captain to be involved, but converting strategy to application is difficult. With fifteen minutes to go, leading 18–12, the team exploded. Brad was superb as his strategies to isolate tiring opposition defenders came to life with his aggressive running. His tactical nous and skill was an outstanding demonstration of an elite player delivering a winning performance in a crucial and defining contest.

Typically, as with all special players, Fittler delivered when it counted; he appeared comfortable with the responsibility of his command, as if this was his destiny.

Defeating New Zealand at Old Trafford is a career highlight, alongside working with the great staff and players we had assembled. I feel truly blessed. In contrast, visiting the New Zealand changeroom after the match and seeing Melbourne Storm teammates Stephen Kearny, Richard Swain and Matt Rua suffering defeat was tough.

- Senior Players

I am often asked where the best players fit into elite settings and how they function as a unit when egos, performances and attitudes collide. At this level, many talented and experienced players would step up to leadership roles.

But being the best athlete does not mean automatic selection as a leader. For example, many players were the best in their position but lacked the aptitude, game maturity or composure to function in a role of seniority. Your best athletes need not be concerned with leadership if it may be detrimental to performance. Let the best perform free of pressure.

"True leaders always practice the Three Rs: respect for self, respect for others and responsibility for actions." Anonymous

- Hierarchy

In settling the senior layers in the squad, respect plays a significant role in deciding the hierarchy. As a coach, observing the dynamic between the differing characters was both interesting and complicated, while the natural order of a hierarchy slowly unfolded.

Considering the depth of senior players in the national team, they eventually settled, and a formidable leadership group emerged. An unwritten pecking order amongst the leadership group grew out of a mutual respect and acknowledgement of how everyone could play a significant part. This pecking order was obvious and functioned in several hierarchical layers with great effect. From a coaching stance, the squad's leadership was simplistic but effective. Although a pecking order took shape, their roles were uncomplicated because of shared responsibility.

## The Role of Captain

Speaking with many senior players with whom I have worked (e.g., Matt Rodwell, Ray Herring, Matt Geyer, Tawera Nikau and Scott Sattler), all mentioned the prestige of being captain, but also the complex nature of the position and dealing with peripheral issues such as media responsibility.

At this level, high achievers dominate the landscape, so even being appointed as captain can hold many challenges, not least gaining acceptance as the patriarch of the squad. Nikau said that holding the captaincy adds pressure and finding the right person who can manage this pressure while not having their performance affected is fundamental to appointment.

Our informal job description of the national captain had many significant aspects, including:

- The ability to hold his playing spot in the squad
- Obvious credibility within the ranks of his peers
- Game-specific intelligence with the ability to change up strategies as demanded
- Public persona reflecting the nation's expectations
- Commanding of respect from stakeholders, spectators and players

Inside the Australian team, Brad Fittler had seemed the logical pick considering he had led his club, state and country numerous times with distinction. But this appointment demanded due respect, particularly for an Australian World Cup squad packed with leaders.

The significant aspects of captaincy when applied to Brad's cache of experience reflected the man, the player and the leader. His playing ability was never in question and he had held his post as an elite player at all levels of the game, performing consistently on the biggest stages throughout his career.

I observed that his personality lent itself to the role, as did many of his deeds as an elite player. He was precise and deliberate in the training environment but very relaxed away from the game. Game time also revealed another side to Brad that was more serious but still relaxed; he provided an air of confidence and calmness for his teammates.

He continually demonstrated that he had the innate ability to manage games that were "on the line," providing tactical nous and applying his skill and guile to winning performances. This was especially so in the 2000 World Cup Final during his half-time address and when he applied those strategies during his second half performance. Aggression at the ruck, dominance and control of tackle, and forward domination were simple but important, while his call to follow his lead was inspiring. He was passionate and emotional but in control.

Brad conveyed a relaxed persona in public and to some it did not reflect the responsibility that goes with the job. His ability to downplay issues in the media was one of his attributes, and he certainly kept everyone guessing. From the public's perspective I can only guess what their perception was of Brad as national captain particularly with past (harmless) indiscretions.

Brad grew into the role and the demands of national captain. His skill with the media came from his relaxed style; nothing seemed to faze him. This is largely true, but I did see another side of Brad inside the team environment where responsibility and care sat high on his list of leadership traits.

Brad built his reputation on his ability and progressed to leadership of the national team — maybe by default. He certainly had paid his dues from a playing perspective, earning every accolade available in the game. Respect does not come cheap while dignity, honour and trust were all part of Brad's manner in earning the right to captain his country. It was truly a pleasure to observe.

## Lessons

Coaching the best of the best at the national level was immensely rewarding. Looking back, I found subtle differences in how these elite players applied themselves and how they managed the pressure of expectation and personal performance.

These elite players demonstrated skill and game sense of a high standard and this certainly challenged our perceptions, delivery and methods as coaches. We had to present incrementally challenging levels of expectation and experience for this very talented playing group.

Our coaching sessions were well planned but lacked the intensity of coaching at club level. It was excusable in some respects because lack of time, injuries and rushed squad preparations are always constraints when coaching a representative team on tour. Being on tour presents concerns of well-being that will impact on their training and game performance if left unattended. Importantly, we scheduled down periods to allow players to disconnect from the group. At home this would occur daily as players finished their duties and headed home. In England, we catered for regular breaks during the two months of preparation, travel and game time.

Selecting the national squad was no easy feat. There were many to be appeased, including the obvious players, selectors, stakeholders and, of course, the media. Piecing together a national team has many moving parts, none more so than the "individual performance over combination" dilemma. For instance, combinations such as half-back and five-eight are crucial to game management. If players are already in those positions at the club or representative level, often an individual will lose out at the selection table.

Another occasion is where selectors will remain loyal and ignore poor form where experience is needed in the squad. This often has a "pay back" effect with the individual rewarding selectors with an outstanding performance. I have used these selection philosophies successfully on many occasions.

- Defining Selections

Selection platforms that provide debate at the selection table include speed, power and the general match fitness of the player. These factors should be considered in the selection process along with attitudinal consideration. This has many connotations in the context of athlete form. For instance, indifferent form can affect the individual's composure, timing and balance, which are all critical to consistent performance. Generally, poor form is easily identified, but understanding the reason in these cases is harder to identify and rectify.

Quite simply put, if the player is not game-fit, they should not be considered. Obviously, there are many cases in which players have been injured and gained selection on reputation — these are very rare cases and at all levels strong consideration should be given to selecting fit players.

- Durability and Toughness

So, what does this mean when considering selections? For me, it is a simple question of comparing the players' efforts in context and contest to others in similar positions. The athletes' efforts, and how they are applied, define the individual in a collision sport. An example is former Australian backrower Gordon Tallis. I consider him to be a durable player who displays the significant attributes (such as toughness) required to play a collision sport. Tallis played without compromise and would aggressively challenge and provoke his opponent with the intent to fluster him. He also knew that by playing with an aggressive style he would be forever a marked man. To me, this only adds another dimension to his persona and prowess, where performance is consistently at the high end of duress and competency.

- Ability and Game Smarts

Intelligence is fundamental and can be discussed at the very basic level of the game. Does the individual know how to apply his skill for specific moments and decisions? Game intensity, pressure and key injuries at crucial times will invariably challenge game sense and the application of match strategy.

Collision sport is demanding and puts the body and mind under duress; it is incredibly unforgiving. Those athletes and players who can deliver performance consistently across long periods of pressure deserve selection.

The process can be complicated or simple, but when we dissect selections by position, combination and consistency of performance, there is much to discuss and consider in a team sense.

- Final Selection

There is no secret formula for selection but picking your "best" squad must be the primary driver in most cases, dependent on what level. Defining the term "best" in the context of your environment needs to be considered before selecting your team.

At the professional level, there are many considerations in the make-up of your team. For instance, analysing the make-up and dynamic of your opponent will influence decisions in the style of game you wish to employ. For example, if your opponent's strength is in their forward play while possessing an obvious power game, then this may necessitate selecting more agile, faster players to employ a wide-attacking game with the intent to tire your bigger opponent.

Conversely, at junior and amateur club level serious consideration is given to selecting talent based on development as distinct from winning. Development in this case means a selection criterion based on athlete potential; winning is secondary. This is just a broad-based example to demonstrate contrasting selection processes between pro and amateur environments.

**Postscript by Onéhunga Mata'uiau** (former Manu Samoa Rugby and World Cup, 1999 representative player; Manu Samoa 7s Captain 1995–1999)

*Steve's description of coaching the elite player resonated with me in many ways, particularly in areas that are different in today's coaching. Looking back now, understanding about youth development and its application to the individual is key. Developing their understanding of the professional needs of today's game is critical. As young players we set goals including representing our country (such a proud moment), but did we really understand the process of achieving such a goal? Today, these processes are embedded in the coaching framework to teach the individual to recognise the task ahead and the benefit of their accomplishment.*

*As an elite player my expectation of the coach was to pass on his knowledge of what was needed to compete at the highest levels of rugby. Much of our knowledge during this period came from our mentors and watching our idols on television. Being self-driven was a key to learning "how to be professional" while fitness took precedence. Personally, I was driven to be the best while the coach facilitated my learning and education of the game — an aspect many fail to recognise as elite coaches.*

*During my career there were areas of my game that I felt were missing. Certainly, the techniques of the wider approach to the game lacked the detail of today's modern game. Coaches during my career (1990s) were more inclined to reinforce the requirement for "mental toughness," forgoing tactical aspects of preparation — certainly not a slight on their competency or coaching ability.*

*When discussing coaching, leadership comes to mind. My coaches from that era often chose players to assist with "leading" the squad. Chosen players were generally senior, had the respect and were highly regarded by their peers and led by example. These players were rugby-intelligent and could recognise our tactical needs and the opposition's weakness. Our leaders were prepared to listen to and value others' input, and work with the head coach and management. They possessed a wider understanding of the game's values.*

*The resources and opportunity today certainly prepare our players better to meet the demands of the modern game — on and off the field. Today's modern coach is a resource of knowledge across man management, rugby and sport science. I only wish this was available during my career.*

# CHAPTER 4

# Coaching the Leaders

"Nearly all men can stand adversity, but if you want to test a man's character, give him power." Abraham Lincoln

As Lincoln may have been suggesting, power or leadership becomes a test of individual resolve and character. The challenge for our leaders is to be calm under pressure and make those decisions that will benefit the team in specific moments. Their actions affect not only themselves but others. The ability of an individual to use power and decision-making skills to advance the team's cause is an indication of true leadership quality.

After twenty-five years of professional coaching I am still constantly challenged in method, application and dynamics in coaching. As coaches, we see firsthand how individuals develop as athletes, personalities and, in some cases, leaders. Seeing the platforms of your teaching being applied in life and competition is very rewarding. As coaches of young, aspiring athletes, we have the opportunity and privilege to contribute to their development of character traits, such as self-confidence, self-awareness and self-control, which at some stage are all tested in competition. This is as much a test for your athletes as it is for you as their coach.

# Mentoring

As a coach, you also need to develop your leadership skills, particularly as a mentor. The role of mentor may sometimes overlap with your role of coach, but in function it will operate quite separately inside the coaching environment. Someone said, "Leadership is about being of service to others, not being served by others. Be a mentor, not a boss." That being said, there must be a line between the role of mentor and just how far this function reaches. Your role is to develop the individual's understanding of well-being as an athlete as being just as important to performance as fitness is. Setting boundaries inside the mentoring function is also key to maintaining a professional working relationship.

Mentoring developed as my sense of self evolved, and maturity and experience provided a broader understanding of others that further developed my coaching scope. That is, as a mentor you recognise the responsibility to care for the individual and the benefit to their overall performance. The importance and influence of mentoring cannot be understated in my development and now as a tool inside the coaching environment.

This chapter is a conversation built from my experiences of dealing with the dynamic of developing your team's leaders as a derivative of discussing the differences and parallels between coaching, mentoring and teaching. My lessons from these experiences provide a glimpse of the importance of self-awareness, self-interest and selflessness as common traits in our leaders.

- Developing Leaders

Building a leadership model for your athletes requires a succession plan that incorporates curriculum-based learning that targets not only the group's development but also those individuals whom you see as potential leaders. There should always be a plan to develop leaders. Committing to leadership is as much a priority in my coaching as developing skill and fitness plans.

Further, adopting a leadership plan for your squad ensures that there is always a link between culture, development and the future.

Succession planning is critical, and it enables a smooth transition between coaching system and the role of senior leaders. A commitment by management should remain fundamental to succession planning with a strategic intent to support leadership development.

Generally, I ensure that three layers of leadership emerge inside the squad. Each layer is represented by selected athletes who have demonstrated qualities of good communication, are willing students and good listeners, or can develop in these areas. Broadly, the bottom layer is the younger athletes, the middle layer is the more experienced and still developing, and the final layer is the prefects or the more senior players. The layers focus on disciplines such as education, transitioning individuals between various functions of leadership and developing their mentoring skills.

- Identifying Leaders

For me, the approach to leading is sharing the role of leadership through a collaborative and engaging manner, rather than hierarchal approaches. To enable this vision as a head coach, delegation of responsibility to the athletes provides a learning environment that reflects ownership and an acknowledgment of trust while developing the individual's ability to lead.

"Knowing your players" is a cliché bandied around the coaching ranks, but it is paramount to the identification, empowerment and selection of your squad's leaders. How I choose a potential leader starts with building a relationship with the intent to understand both the simplicities and complexities of the individual. As coach, you have an ideal opportunity to realise what personal, social or other areas may influence the individual's performance and selection as a team leader. Importantly, a defined standard of performance must remain constant for peer acceptance and for the individual to maintain their status as a leader.

A squad leader's roles vary in the context of the coach's needs. One significant function for the senior leader is to decipher coaching strategies to the wider group. This is not only a critical aspect of team coaching but also imperative for performance, stability and testing your leader's development.

There is no avoiding a commitment to developing leaders in your squad if you want consistency of performance and success. From my experience, your leaders represent and reflect your coaching philosophies, principles and systems that ultimately drive performance.

- Coach-Leader Relationship

My experiences have relied heavily on strong relationships with my senior players to guide, refine methods of delivery and build team harmony. This relationship with your leaders is as productive as the complexity, maturity and acceptance of these roles. As I have matured as a coach, my understanding of individuals and their behaviour as athletes has enabled a more productive working relationship. As I outwardly became more confident and accepted the function of teacher and mentor, I became less threatening to the athletes. Further, the importance of experience in the teaching role while also having a willingness to share wisdom is critical to the learning environment. This includes drawing on professional expertise from outside your system.

The ongoing development of the coach-leader relationship plays such an important part in being an effective and productive coach. Understanding your leaders should be a matter of due diligence, and it is fundamental to isolating any barriers that could affect the team's performance. Various forms of profiling have been beneficial to finding the connections between those characteristics of your leaders and your philosophies that will enable the coach-leader relationship. With this knowledge, the complexities of coaching become more apparent as you juggle coaching responsibilities, mentoring and maintenance of these relationships with your team leaders.

Player-Coach Profile

The importance of knowing the athlete is critical to offset potential issues arising from the relationship. Building a relationship on trust, care and integrity complements learning but also increases your understanding of the athlete's expectations. Forging a bond also ensures that the overarching process between the athlete and coach is effective in enhancing performance.

I recommend finding common links from social, personal and performance as key to opening the gate between player and coach. I also recommend not being too complex in discussions. You want to get to know the person. Additionally, you should keep the manner of communication as basic as your environment demands. Developing rapport is the priority. Building the specifics of any key role of leadership can be done as you begin to establish a greater understanding of the individual. The key is to find ways of connecting with the player to form common links that enable the relationship to develop.

Conversely, at the elite level of the game, I recommend a comprehensive profiling process with the individual, which may require external facilitators. This is to ensure the intended relationship between coach and athlete is to assist performance while the use of an external specialist ensures a wider support for the athlete (i.e., their well-being).

The bond between player and coach is essential for team performance, while the link between coach, player and the leaders can loosely be defined by the maturity of that relationship, how the role is prioritised and how the individual may perceive that role within the team.

Profiling an individual at a junior level is simply to develop their skill sets at one end of the profile spectrum, while developing a relationship with their parents (influences) and the child. The illustration below demonstrates the balancing act and dynamic the coach and player undertake to enhance the relationship.

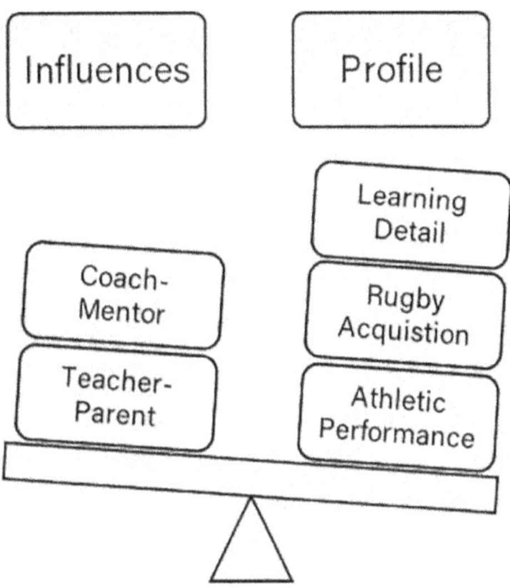


- Leaders

What do I look for in a leader? What defines a leader and sets them apart from others? I select leaders whose character traits offer a value set that others gravitate toward – not fear, dominance or aggression but openness, supportiveness and trust. I recognise individuals who have emotional intelligence and display an ability to manage delegated leadership functions in a non-threatening manner.

There are many examples from my career when I quickly recognised players that demonstrated leadership skills; their influence carries inspiration and a maturity of character. Not all are elite, but all have similar characteristics. They have sport-specific intelligence and respect for their peers, they are effective communicators and they see their role as working between the coach and the squad.

Within this group, I have seen players with various character traits who have operated as leaders. For example, there are those who lead as captains and possess the all-round approach, including tactical nous. They lead by action and use their intelligence and influence in a strategic manner to benefit the team and themselves.

## Intelligence

While I was coaching at the Gold Coast Seagulls (Australian Rugby League), it was obvious the players actively listened and responded well to Ray Herring (former Brisbane Broncos and Gold Coast Seagulls professional). As an experienced professional held in high regard by his peers, he had a steadying influence on the group. Ray's influence was critical in key aspects of providing accurate insights into the team's character, understanding the group's needs and flagging performance flaws.

His game-specific intellect and group acceptance of the leadership role provided a direct link to the team's psyche, which was invaluable to steering performance and managing failure. During this period, there were many tough and challenging times for the club, including a poor season. Having the support of senior leaders during this period provided not only a shared responsibility but also a controlled view of performance, largely driven by Ray's maturity and realistic perspective.

Ray commented, *"Personally, the most important relationship was with the coach. Early in my career a coach said he didn't care if we liked him; what he was concerned about was whether he could teach and develop us as rugby league players and people. For me, this makes a good coach."*

My relationship with Ray provided a platform for my own learning, particularly in areas of team management and refining my communication skills. I was young, inexperienced and lacked a maturity at the professional end of sport. I was learning on the run and to have senior players offer their support was much needed. Upon reflection, I should have relied more on the team leaders and staff to offset my inexperience and to support my development as a head coach.

## Perfectionist

As a new franchise in the National Rugby League (1998), the Melbourne Storm had assembled arguably one of the most formidable playing groups of the modern era. They secured established leaders and internationals in Glen Lazarus, Tawera Nikau, Robbie Kearns and Stephen Kearney. All of these men are fantastic leaders and contributed massively to managing the squad during this period while gaining the ultimate reward of a national premiership (1999).

Tawera Nikau (former New Zealand international; NRL Melbourne Storm premiership winner) was the ultimate professional who had represented his country many times before he stepped into his contract at Melbourne. If there was such a thing as a natural leader, Tawera was close to it. His ability and character complemented the playing group. He was often the joker in the pack until it was game time. He was one of the most competitive players I have come across, and I later worked with him again in the UK Super League. His aggressive style was full of energy and guile and his "never take a backward step" attitude was a perfect foil for a squad that contained inexperienced players.

My relationship with Tawera took many forms, including formal and informal chats around the team's attitude and mental toughness. Tawera was a student of the game and he used every available resource to enhance performance at an individual and team level. He was targeted in his approach, starting with study of his game-evaluation — a standard tool I used that included offensive and defensive areas that required corrections and notations on attainment of match targets.

He would often source interpretation of analysis and relationship with performance before actioning small areas of his game across the weekly preparation sessions. Aside from his talent, his attention to detail of performance was arguably his point of difference.

Tawera said, *"I looked forward to our weekly review sessions at the Melbourne Storm where Steve would constantly challenge me from many different perspectives, in particular my role as a leader and how to influence others within our wider squad."*

Tawera was acutely aware of the foundation of elite performance and would regularly discuss routine and habits that may have been conflicting with team performance or his own ideal performance state.

He was a fantastic athlete with a mature outlook that was infectious in the group and he was dedicated to peak performance. Winning was non-negotiable while losing was met with disdain, which set standards that impacted positively on others in the squad. He demanded excellence.

Both personally and professionally, Tawera has had a huge impact on my development as a coach. His leadership style on and off the field was defined by his actions, standards and values of excellence, dedication and commitment to performance. Those obvious indicators of leadership were evident in the way he conducted himself in team functions, how he utilised his study of opponents for squad understanding in team meetings and the respect he had for fellow athletes.

As a coach, I was overwhelmed by his commitment to be the best in each action; every movement culminates in a desire to win. Much was designed to motivate and inspire his teammates — a true quality of a champion. His support for others was obvious.

The relationship we built was served by an expectation of mutual benefit that I have continued to foster in my coaching.

- The Captain

Nominating a captain for the Warrington Wolves in the UK Super League was my greatest challenge. The club has a long history of success and many champion players have filled the captain's role admirably. There were many gifted players who were arguably qualified to assume the role of captain. During this period, many complex issues surrounded the captain's appointment, not least the pressure to find a person with the right fit and qualities to match the club's brand, stakeholders and supporters — not to mention the media.

John Clarke and Lee Briers (both internationals) were eminently qualified to lead the club. These players had obvious qualities as leaders of men and the ability to assess and transfer information to players in training and matches. Either of them would have been capable appointments and no doubt led the team with distinction.

In the end, I chose Australian Matt Rodwell, who had experience in several professional rugby league clubs in Australia (Newcastle, St. George, Western Reds and Penrith). This was an appointment that became somewhat of a challenge as a difficult season unfolded.

Matt was a key veteran signing and unquestioned as a professional. He was a champion guy — personable, with a young family, and an experienced leader. This point was defining in his selection as captain. He had previously captained sides and had a clear understanding of the role and expectations.

It was unfortunate that Captain Matt was continually undermined by the events surrounding an underperforming team facing relegation. This placed a strain on our relationship, which added to the burden of leadership. His qualities as a leader were tested many times as we managed a club in crisis.

What further enhanced my opinion of Matt was how he managed one particular incident that involved his family. This event further demonstrated the significance of appointing a captain of character and resilience. Sadly, the club did little to support Matt or the team during this period — a reflection on the "state" of the organisation, I contest.

This is arguably the worst moment I have witnessed in my career and it reflected poorly on the club, spectators and rugby brand. Matt and his family were pelted with coins by the Warrington supporters as he left the changerooms after a run of defeats. I will never understand this treatment of any player, let alone a club captain who was a quality person who was going above and beyond for the club. This was a defining moment and one that influenced my decision to quit as head coach.

His loyalty and character never wavered during this period as he motivated his squad while continuing to play with an injury that only management knew about. He was leading an underperforming squad on behalf of a club struggling on and off the field.

### Lessons

Teamwork, being selfless, and caring remain constant in my coaching environment — I purposefully build these traits as elements of effective teams. Teamwork is the key. How you attend to the function of teamwork underlines your ability as coach. The skill of building "team" is the key and can be challenging on several fronts — none more so than breaking down existing or perceived barriers.

I have referenced key areas evident in leaders, such as self-awareness (empathy), selflessness (relationship) and selfishness (team first). These traits were on display at some level inside these leaders' actions and behaviour, while all possessed an integrity and respect for their profession.

## Self-awareness

The enormity of leadership and its responsibilities is in every decision you make as a coach. In a team sport such as rugby, our senior athletes sacrifice their needs for the greater good of the team.

Leaders have an ability to adjust how they communicate and engage to be positively perceived by their peers in challenging moments. Be it in a formal or casual meeting between the players, they share common characteristics in how they convey messages and how they need to be perceived by the wider group — that is, in a positive and supportive manner where there is a shared vision, demanding openness and clarity for the team's sake.

Players who were under scrutiny for indifferent form were openly supported even though they may have contributed to a losing performance. This form of empathy and affirmation was always displayed in these circumstances, both in individual and group scenarios. These affirmative displays of support positively influenced the players and performance. However, standards and outcomes were still an essential part of the team's goals. Even though there was positive support for the individual, the team came first. In these moments I saw how leaders demonstrated loyalty, trust and an empathy for those players. However, at the same time, they stayed loyal to achieving the best results to preserve the team's position in the standings.

The empathy they displayed came from an understanding of how they would feel or act in a similar circumstance and how they wished to be treated, which in turn governed their behaviour and actions toward others. These leaders all appeared to be closely connected to their emotions and displayed maturity beyond their years in understanding human response and feelings.

- Selflessness

As coach, teams that are prepared to sacrifice possess the foundation to success. This can be seen through the positive emotions and reactions where "team" is placed before individual need. "We" and "us" describe their outlook while "I" and "me" are rarely used.

This characteristic of sacrifice may sound out of place in professional sport environments, but in context has great influence, particularly on camaraderie. The leaders I have referenced in this chapter all underlined their own awareness of mateship and those bonds on which team sport is built. These leaders were always quick to shift attention from duty to building relationships through social and other recreational pursuits. Performing at the elite level was important to them as professionals, but they were always very conscious of downtime as a part of their weekly routines.

In training and matches they led from the front with their attention and focus driven by winning, while off the field they were very conscious of being part of the group. They seemed different in how they engaged with the squad with an intention to be more affable, humorous and engaging.

One of the most selfless acts I have witnessed at the elite level of rugby league was Andrew Johns (Rugby League Immortal) accepting his role in the Australian Kangaroos World Cup squad (2000) as a hooker and not in his favoured halfback role. As an on-field marshal and tactician, Andrew was completely selfless in acknowledging the selection process. A player of quality and standing in the game, he displayed maturity, respect and humility for the decision and completely bought into the "team first" mentality.

- Selfishness

This characteristic resonated amongst all the leaders I have mentioned, but it has several meanings. They were not selfish in how they conducted themselves, but it was obvious that each leader possessed the ability to be "about themselves" in how they prepared as athletes. Individuals may assume leadership roles within the team, but, ultimately, they are expected to perform consistently to not only maintain their position but also hold their role as a leader. With the threat of their position being challenged, selfish traits may surface, and the bias will shift toward themselves. This is not to be confused with ego.

They were concerned for others in their understanding of the team aspect of preparation, but when it came to their own performance, they were acutely aware of achieving their goals. This reaction is not unique in professional settings considering each is responsible for their own performance, but it is unique in the context of being aware of individual empathy and securing bonds. "Relationships aren't designed for selfish individuals," someone once said, and I agree.

Chapter 5

# Experience of Success

The Melbourne Storm of the National Rugby League (NRL) is one of the most successful sporting franchises in Australia but it is also one of the youngest. The club's ability to make the final series is remarkable and a testimony to "success breeds success!" Their organisation thrives as a collective sharing the common traits of respect and humility.

In my experience, success is derived from the quality of your athletes and the ability of your coaching staff to create an environment that is single-mindedly aimed at achieving results. I was fortunate to coach at an organisation that was building a club from people who knew how to prepare, realise and sustain success both on and off the field.

Admittedly, much is required for sustained success where governance, finance and recruitment layers of the club are key — but the evidence is overwhelming in the Melbourne Storm.

The demand for success began in the very first staff meeting I attended in October 1997, which was convened by General Manager John Ribot (former Brisbane Broncos CEO) at the Herald Sun building in Melbourne. The language was foreign in some respects, littered with an acknowledgment that anything is achievable with the right people, suitable resources and hard work without compromise.

The following account conveys success as gained through a combination of experienced leaders, a driven coaching staff and a talented playing roster devoid of distraction. This period had a profound effect on my development while some of those lessons are still evident in my coaching environment today. I learnt that a coach should:

1.  Be aware that tough decisions will challenge player loyalty.
2.  Understand the necessity that one voice is key for clarity and consistency of message.
3.  Remember that winning is derived from a player-driven culture.

Although these elements are not explored in depth, the following background material indirectly mentions their relationship with achieving success and key lessons from my experience.

## Background

Our home, Olympic Park Stadium, became a fortress thanks to a very handy squad of players assembled by senior executives and Head Coach Chris Anderson. Combined with this squad and astute management, we quickly became a success and gained a loyal spectator base that still exists today.

Chris came to Melbourne as a very experienced and successful coach, having won premierships in the northern and southern hemispheres. Although easy-going, his style was based on loyalty and respect that resonated in a very willing, settled and driven playing group.

For me, Chris's greatest attribute was his ability to find the balance between character, performance and (developing) culture. This was one of the critical areas of our program; as staff we challenged the squad's development with an intent to maximise performance by aligning their expectations of realising success. Character was represented in the standards we (the organisation) set while culture was driven by honesty and respect between staff and our clients, stakeholders and opponents. Notwithstanding the quality of athlete and squad assembled in this period (1998-2000), our program demanded success.

## Coaching Model

The structure was simplistic and effective, but comparatively under-resourced if it were to be attempted in today's high-tech environments. It was important that staff member skill sets and styles complemented each other, while our experience could fill any voids or tasks in the structure. Multifaceted staff members are invaluable and a must in a dynamic environment such as professional coaching. Our staff were dynamic and adapted easily to obscure challenges, which resulted in reward.

Our functions were clearly defined. The head coach was devoted to team strategy. As assistant coach I managed the analysis that underpinned strategy as well as individual remedial and positional work. Our skill-development coach, Greg Brentnall (former Australia, New South Wales and Canterbury Bankstown player), managed generic practice, which is often undervalued. The crucial part was that our feeder club (Brisbane Norths) was aligned in principle with our philosophies and led by astute coaches Mark Murray (former Eastern Suburbs Sydney head coach; former Queensland State of Origin representative) and Anthony Griffin who would become Brisbane Broncos and Penrith head coach.

As a body of staff, there was a singularity in our alignment and goals. We operated with aligned clarity, while the athletes fed from an efficient program led by astute executives and coaches.

- Systems

As Chris often said, "It's a simple game and we shouldn't complicate it." He talked about the game in layman's terms, which is a win for both players and staff.

Defensively, his strategy was to control the ruck, while the system outside of the ruck would take care of itself if the ruck was in order. From this concept we managed to implement several defence styles that became the platform for our success. Not a lot of credit was afforded to our defence, but the players certainly acknowledged the importance of honing our defensive structures.

Our attacking philosophy was primarily based on flatline or playing on the gain line and striving for continuity with numbers pushing up to support the ball carrier. We would spend hours perfecting the art of speed in these key systems. Power, accuracy and control were fundamental to the mechanics of our skill program, while commitment, desire and aggression held our attitude to account. Strategically, our match preparation was based on our strengths that targeted specific anomalies of our opponent. This approach served us well.

- Fitness

Our game style was to dominate and control with aggression. To achieve this style, our physicality was driven by power and speed, as were our muscular endurance and functional fitness. Our conditioning guru, Aaron Salisbury, would map our preseason workloads further into the competition phase of the season before dropping training loads mid-year. This was designed to benefit the team the further we went into the final series.

Keeping athletes on the field and medically fit managed by very proactive support staff (physiotherapist Tony Ayoub) were massive contributors to our early success.

- Method

It was important for early week sessions to be full contact and this was maintained throughout the season. At the time, this practice contradicted many sports science philosophies of shaping your training week, whereby work volumes and contact-type sessions were minimised for fear of injury. This format was another critical area to our program as the players were challenged with game-specific speed under collision threat to enhance applied skill.

- Selections

Picking weekly teams was generally settled over Monday morning reviews. There was a loose format to our meetings and debate would hinge on reports from our medical and fitness departments. Most debate was about training volume, time and physical contact limits for those with soft-tissue injuries and those who could and could not train.

While injury was a consideration to selection, on occasion Chris ignored the professionals and sought advice from the player. He expected the elite players to know their bodies, and I cannot recall a time we were left short from carrying an injured player into a game. That is a testimony to Chris's experience and ability to back his players.

## Culture

Many have asked what the culture was like at Melbourne because it was such a successful environment. Defining culture can be difficult. Sure, there are the consistent elements that underpin success such as belief systems, value sets, and principles and philosophies, but personalities largely dictate and influence the fundamentals of culture. Principled people finish first.

The character of a successful organisation is easily identifiable by high-achieving athletes and aligned business goals. Conflict and debate are common, but egos are kept in check. Today, when I do not see the interplay of these characteristics, I am concerned for ownership and performance. The illustration below summarises my perception of culture, where "principles" (applied operation standards) sit at the core of success.

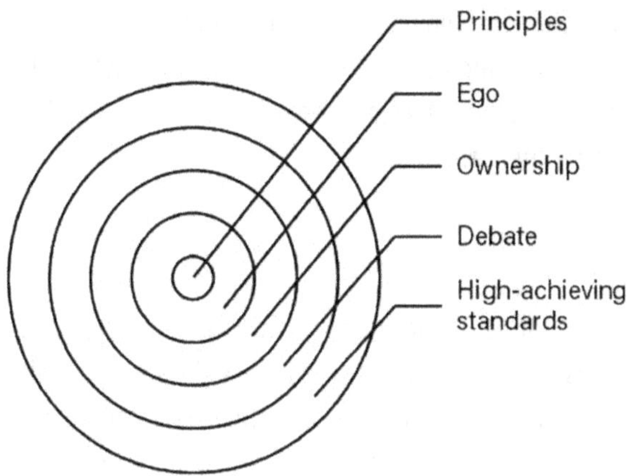


Melbourne Storm was no different. We managed the balance between player ego and what was best for the team. Ego is a necessary element in high-performing teams and should be enabled but managed — there is a difference. We had very good athletes who respected that the boundaries, standards and values were not to be compromised. Delegating responsibility to our senior playing group was central in managing a culture in which players owned their actions and were responsible to the team expectations. Self-perpetuating ego was not to be tolerated while team first mentality was unquestioned.

- Values

From top to bottom, the organisation promoted a culture of "team." Our senior player group became the head coach's mouthpiece in times of challenge. Our core values that operated at the heart of the playing group — such as care, respect and support — were fundamental elements of our success. This is where the selection of your squad is critical and having the "right personalities" in your club is necessary to achieve success. Consideration of how you address values and what the group represents is a must.

There must be a premise of what the club conveys as a set of standards and principles. Early discussion each year, largely led by the senior player group, was fundamental for defining image and acceptable behaviour. Setting boundaries and standards is an integral component to realising the season's expectations underpinned by a defined set of values that guide key actions and decisions of the team.

## Belonging

I must say that I struggled for many years after I left Melbourne. My time at the club has never been matched as far as the sense of belonging and support. The club encouraged innovation, and staff were given latitude to explore what would make us better. This led to a sense of support and a willingness from the coaching staff and players to listen to new ideas.

Obviously, after a successful season debut (1998) we knew this was an exceptional group of athletes defined by willing students and complemented by a blend of strong characters and skill.

Generally, our coaching environment was creative, competitive and purposeful, but as with any coaching group we had the odd clash with players as we strived for performance consistency in training and competition. Many debates were concerned with not attaining performance goals (i.e., what we had set as a goal for team win-loss ratio at specific moments of the season).

To rectify this, we were challenged to realign our coach-player alignment. Understanding the process was fundamental to our game plan and, generally, after this type of process of rectification, positive outcomes would result. After losing we never panicked, which is testimony to our use of experienced players and the creation of a stable environment that was player-led. However, we did panic if our processes were defective, misunderstood or not transferred into games.

When we raised the bar for expectation, the players were equal to the challenge. We were continually looking for precision across all facets of the team. Precise repetition and being able to transfer our training habits into a match was fundamental to our success. Individual acceptance of high standards drove their performance, but more importantly it set the standard of training and their preparation.

## Grand Final, National Rugby League (NRL)

1999 is a fond memory for all of us. Winning the NRL Grand Final in only our second year of existence was an enormous achievement and will probably never be matched.

Going into our final rounds of the season, we continued to adjust our squad as the players struggled with the pressure of expectation. One of our biggest hurdles was injuries to key players and knowing the team had peaked early and our best performances were behind us. In addition, we had new combinations in crucial positions that at times affected our continuity, structure and execution.

Due to injury, we had used various combinations in key playmaker roles. Other position changes had also been made that were unavoidable and the impact on performance was unknown.

Limping into the final series, our only real hope lay with our experienced campaigners Glen Lazarus, Tawera Nikau and Stephen Kearney, and an in-form halfback Brett Kimmorley (voted best on field in the Grand Final). The reality of the team at this moment was our best rugby was behind us, which hit home when we lost to North Sydney in our last season fixture. Not a good way to enter the final series campaign.

To say our coaching staff were challenged is an understatement. The work had been done and after ten months we certainly were not going to go without a fight, which is what happened in 1998 after two back-to-back final series losses. One aspect we were aware of was the resolve within a cluster of seasoned internationals, many who had played State of Origin fixtures and Grand Finals previously.

Our approach to all games whether finals or competition fixtures was to create a settled environment that allowed space between coach and player while support was available if required. We supported familiarity, routine and habit as we went about building confidence rather than trying to fix issues at this late stage of the year. Our process and tactics never wavered, and we backed our power game led by our forwards to pave the way through the final series and into the Grand Final. There was nothing fancy about the game plan, but it isolated our strengths.

Coupled with the pressure of being a new franchise, this team managed the unthinkable and won the Grand Final, sending the club into rugby league folklore.

## World Club Challenge, UK (2000)

After the 1999 Grand Final, the squad was reassembled, minus very experienced players who had either moved on or retired. It is true about the hangover from Grand Finals and we could tell in our preparation that this team was no different. There was an abundance of talent (new and old) but there was a definite sense of overconfidence that wasn't backed by our preparation. At best, it lacked the consistency of attitude and application of previous preseasons.

What this squad lacked in preparation was made up by a skilful group. The crispness and combinations were still evident, and that sense of overconfidence was actually needed. As a coaching staff, we were still in an enviable position as we entered the 2000 season.

Realigning player attitudes, resetting their goals and attending to the World Club Challenge were all part of our season planning. The NRL season commenced in March, so our planning was geared toward fine-tuning the squad at this stage — not playing a World Club Cup Final! It is difficult coming off the back of a Grand Final because of the "high" the players experience and the adjustment to "business as usual" when the life of a professional rugby player resumes. Did we adjust much of our planning? No. The key was rest and active recovery for our senior players while the younger players continued with the routines of preseason preparation.

The timing of the World Club Challenge has always created conjecture as both the UK Super League and the NRL seasons are very much in preseason mode at that time. The timing was also a major hurdle from a season preparation perspective, as we worked outside of our normal seasonal routines.

The game reflected the depth of talent at the club and the cohesion of the group even without big game players from 1999 (Lazarus retired; Nikau had moved on). The game had its moments, as we claimed the title of World Club champions against the UK Super League title holders St. Helens.

## Lessons

I had developed as a coach in many ways, including gaining a greater appreciation of fluidity and being adaptable. Prior to the Melbourne Storm, my coaching was about the detail rather than the essence, emotion or feel for the game. The mechanics of the game had eroded my innocence and the foundation of my coaching to a point that my focus had shifted to the science of the game, to the detriment of my philosophy.

Through the staff and players, I was provided a lesson of applying knowledge with relevance, while there was also a reawakening about never losing sight of the player as central to my work. Accordingly, you should always consider your surrounding environment and the people who provide the support as critical to the success of your program. As an example: our work was only as good as the skill of the staff and how each contributed and applied their intellect as part of the collective.

- Knowledge, Context and Relevance

You can have statistics and the best analysis systems in the game, but data must provide meaning to the player's performance.

Data analysis can be misleading without context and reference to the season, match plans and training outcomes. Links between all facets of your program and game deliverables for analysis must be evident to be truly representative of a given performance or action.

I try to find areas of training and competition that will provide a platform for improvement. Data, on the other hand, is the "raw stat," such as performance rates, time and percentage of territory, and general statistics such as errors. Combined, both data and analysis can be fantastic tools in supporting the player's and the team's development.

My view is to contextualise data in a manner that challenges an action, moment or measured objective of performance. For example, looking at the action and moments prior to an error can provide context to the mistake. Was the error unforced? Was it a result of other variables? Much of my approach to data is driven by enabling the team's response to precision and execution, while critiquing my system demands a deeper investigation of individual alignment and applied actions. System errors can occur through a misunderstanding of a set play that leads to an error. A fundamental error (e.g., a missed tackle) can be attributed to an individual action that was an unforced error.

- Staff and Relationships

The closeness of our playing group at Melbourne grew from the isolation of the team in the first instance. We turned that isolation into bonds that existed on and off the field between the players, staff and their families. Many of those bonds exist today and prove the merit of using character and personality as a key criterion in hiring people into elite environments.

Finding the right fit relies on understanding the personality of potential staff or athletes and the type of business. This approach is essential for elite sports where character and culture are aligned. For example, character in this instance refers to individual personality as well as the organisations. For instance, the "how and what" of preparing a high-performing squad requires a sense of "self" or identity that enables motivation and underpins performance. Developing a "culture" requires an identity that is built on shared values and beliefs that align and, ultimately, drive performance.

What came out of this approach at Melbourne resulted in consistency of approach, collegial thinking and aligned personalities.

- Emotion and Performance

Because of the direct dealings with individuals and groups in your preparation, winning and losing is inevitable. Emotions attached to those outcomes must be dealt with and understood. Understanding how those emotions and relationships will better serve performance was fundamental in Melbourne's rise. This was achieved through the bonds established between the players, staff members and families. The intimacy of Melbourne in social and work settings provided a glimpse of people's attitudes and responses to winning and losing and, more importantly, how we recovered from failure.

Although not validated scientifically, I have no doubt that we were leading the field in professional sport at the time by conducting performance monitoring sessions with our players. This process was designed to assist the individual to recognise specific emotional states and relationships to training and performance outcomes. Tracking staff welfare and the athletes' physical and emotional state provides information that can influence training and competitive performance. Today we refer to this area as "well-being."

- People Before Football

Recruiting players and staff who have strong values and principles is essential when bringing a team together. If you want success, select the right people. From working closely with senior executives at Melbourne, it was obvious that the "people first policy" was significant in all initial signings. This was not manufactured, but it was a deliberate approach derived from the executives and a head coach who cared about the immediate perceptions of the club's stakeholders and the club's future.

These guys knew about building a team on the cornerstone of character and culture whereby standards, performance and strong value sets provide the platform for success. All had played at the highest levels of the game and experienced success as coaches and administrators.

**Postscript by Matt Geyer** (former captain Melbourne Storm and NRL premiership winner; NSW State of Origin representative; former Western Reds professional)

*At the elite level, success is defined in the win-loss column, but at local and developmental levels, I have seen success in many different ways: being happy that a young player can now attend training because his single mother has found someone to care for other siblings or having a junior player make a strong tackle and look to me with pride and ask, "Matt, did you see that?" Those moments rank as highly as any win and are equally important to the success of a football club.*

*Further, coach-player relationship and team culture do not have to be mutually exclusive; rather, it's the opposite. Investing in your players and taking an interest in their lives may be just as important as taking them through a tough field session or showing them how to improve through video analysis.*

*I often speak to young men and explain why I invest in the relationship side of coaching. While my motivation is to build strong bonds, mutual benefit may be gained in working as a group and building a favourable win-loss column.*

*As a senior player it is vital you provide the link between the coaching staff and playing group without jeopardising your presence or relationship with either. I always felt my role as captain was to ensure each player was welcome and valued. I would often invite a new player to my home and let them know our club cares. While this type of act won't win premierships, it is an important cog in the machine. While it is nice to have a captain who is well spoken and can deliver the right words at the right time, I feel the best form of leadership is to lead with actions. If, as a leader, you want to keep your players accountable for their actions, you must display those actions also.*

My first Head Coach role, aged 18 - U15 Emerald Tigers; Rundle Park 1981

Reward - Head Coach High Performance; Western Force debutants
Mike McDonald; Carlo Tizzano. NIB Stadium, Perth, Aus., 2019

Apprentice - Player Coach Southern Suburbs; Davies Park Brisbane 1988

Novice - Player Coach Milton Keynes UK 1989

Learning opportunity - invaluable lessons from respected rugby
league dignitaries led by Peter Corcoran (AM); Dennis Ward and
Brad Levey - National Coaching Conference, Ballina, NSW, 1992

Hardwork - Assistant Coach, Melbourne Storm
NRL Grand final; Homebush Stadium, Sydney 1999. Alongside
myself: Michael Anderson; Greg & Mark Brentnall

Celebrate - Assistant Coach, Australian Kangaroos, World
Cup victory v NZ, 2000. Old Trafford, England
Back - Rob Kearns; Scott Hill & Brett Kimmorley; Middle - myself
& Tony Ayoub; Front - Aaron Salisbury & Steve Litvensky

Melbourne Storm connection - Steve Litvensky; myself;
Tony Ayoub; Chris Anderson; Aaron Salisbury enjoy World
Cup Victory - Old Trafford, Manchester UK; 2000

Reflect - Head Coach, Warrington Super League UK; 2002

Concern - Performance Director, Defence Coach; Six Nations Rugby,
England v Scotland; Twichenham Stadium; London - England 2005

# SECTION THREE

# The Downside of Elite Coaching: Discussing Conflict, Values and Professionalism

*As a player, the expectations you require from a coach have changed over time. Personally, I just wanted a coach who knew MY game and didn't pigeonhole me.*

*Every player has diverse characteristics on the field, and a coach that identifies and harnesses those could help me prepare and perform well.*

*The coaches I always felt helped his team improve and individuals develop were the ones who never forgot the fundamentals first and foremost.*

*In saying that, there were areas of preparation where I sought counsel. For example, position and game expectation require a marriage between player, team and coach.*

*Although I had personal goals, I was a member of a team that required alignment with overarching performance outcomes. This area in particular was a collaboration guided by the coach, often resulting in debate.*

- Scott Sattler (former NRL premiership winner; Queensland State of Origin representative; former Gold Coast, South Queensland Crushers and Penrith Panthers professional)

Coaching is dynamic, contains emotional challenges and uses the uncertainty of winning as central. Conflict has many forms in professional coaching, no more so than those debates and challenges that arise from expectation. The breakdown of relationship between staff, athlete and structure conflict where athlete-team perception of performance collides.

Scott Sattler indicates the balancing act between coach and athlete where emotion, performance and outcomes intersect with potential for conflict. This is but one area of professional organisations where conflict exists.

This section provides a glimpse of the negative side to coaching that can be personally devastating, potentially career-ending and emotionally scarring.

My discussion focuses on several experiences that raise questions about my ability as a coach to detach from the emotion and trauma of failure while maintaining an ability to reflect in a manner conducive to professional growth. In contrast, I have challenged senior executives for their part, the function and relevance of the coaching model and the significance of due diligence.

A secondary component of this section highlights the fragility of professional coaching and the balancing act we undertake to manage the functions of our role without imposing prejudice or bias. I talk about the role of head coach being split between managing the emotional and functional needs of the athlete while meeting the board's expectations and satisfying your own personal goals.

Considering the nature of these accounts and the reference to individuals, it should be noted that these are my interpretations and observations. In saying this, these accounts are a testimony to the challenges that confront professional coaches as winning consumes all facets of the organisation.

# CHAPTER 6

# Dealing with Conflict

Many of our concerns as coaches arise from our own neglect of challenging our methodologies, structures or communication processes. Conflict arises from the undiscussed, the unprepared or from the "head in the sand" approach to addressing the concerns in your program. As a result, when planning is challenged, responsibility is often misrepresented, diverted or, in some cases, neglected.

Encouraging debate and constant interplay amongst the coaching staff is essential to finding an aligned program and consistent message. Challenging and debating in a constructive manner can be rewarding and positive if the process is managed in a collaborative style with an intent to build respectful relationships. The more staff and athletes are encouraged to discuss, challenge and debate aspects of their environment the more likely there is clarity of function while performance outcomes are consistently achieved.

In this discussion, I have used my interpretations to explain how ineffective communication can lead to staff conflict, disharmony and a loss of purpose. Robust discussions are commonplace and necessary to maintain the balance of mutual respect between staff in a functional organisation. A lack of openness and transparency is a result of poor communication processes that invariably lead to failure. The significance of open communication cannot be understated as a tool for consistency of staff approach and, ultimately, performance.

In the coaching environment, confidence gained through transparent communication is essential for productive teams. This process also provides a means of avoiding negativity and conflict. As a coach, you must acknowledge and accept that debate is healthy for productive planning. Conversely, unforeseen or unmanaged concerns can be a catalyst for disharmony, disruption and poor performance. In my role as a professional coach, I have learnt to observe group behaviours to ensure that healthy debate is supported.

The occasions when debate is perceived as unconstructive or intrusive can become irreparable if left unattended. Throughout my career there have been many incidents of this nature, many of which were borne from an immaturity of staff and structure. In this case, time, leadership and constant guidance is required until staff acknowledge debate as a productive tool.

Working inside a conflicted mode of practice obviously dampens the quality of staff exchanges and may jeopardise an individual's respect for his workplace. Accordingly, it is very hard to be positive or maintain a sense of purpose inside this type of environment.

Robust discussion provides a constant challenge to keeping your program fluid and ensuring material is fresh and adaptable to the needs of performance. Constantly meeting to discuss areas of concern will ensure the system anomalies are flagged and addressed. Regular meetings also build bonds that are necessary and fundamental to the foundation of coaching.

The following account is of a system that was challenged at many levels, including by poor communication. Resulting factions between coaches and senior executives contributed to a loss of direction, while my sense of purpose and job satisfaction plummeted. These events, including my development as a coach, still hold me to account in many ways.

## Setting

In 1993 as a young professional coach, I joined the Gold Coast Seagulls (Australian Rugby League) that was populated by experienced staff and worked in a fantastic facility that instantly felt secure. I held two positions: assistant first team coach and second head coach. It was an exciting appointment for a rookie coach.

This was one of the most challenging periods of my career. At thirty, I was young for a professional coach, and I soon found that I was ill-equipped to manage the challenges that manifested during my tenure. Apart from the well-documented financial management issues of the organisation, many of the concerns were borne out of the proposed "Super League" concept, which would challenge the rugby league fraternity, including player contract terms and conditions.

My appointment came about by respected fitness guru Billy Johnston (former Southern Suburbs, Brisbane; St. George Dragons, Gold Coast Giants and Canterbury Bankstown professional - NSWRL premiership winner), who had provided a recommendation to then CEO Greg Bandiera (former Newtown Jets; Balmain Tigers and Eastern Suburbs - NSWRL Grand Final winner). I was working with the Illawarra Steelers (ARL) at the time, but I soon accepted a contract offer to join the Gold Coast club. As part of their vision, highly respected coach Graeme Murray (former Illawarra, Hunter Mariners, Leeds Rhinos, Sydney Roosters and North Queensland Cowboys and NSW State of Origin head coach) was also approached to build a consistently high-performing club.

Unfortunately, much of what had been planned would not eventuate due to various changes, including a fast-approaching "Super League" reality and the resignation of the CEO, which derailed the organisation's vision. This was the beginning of a tough tenure at the club, and it provided a reality check to my naive perception of being a professional coach.

- Football Department

When I arrived, many of the structures and support systems were in place, and additional development of the facility was to be implemented as part of the club's long-term vision. The previous coaching regime had attempted to modernise the coaching structure, including introducing a comprehensive analysis system. In some way, today's analysis systems can be attributed to the Gold Coast's modern thinking on the game.

The club's athletic and development section was filled with experienced personnel, all with extensive backgrounds in their fields. Their work, as within most professional sporting arenas, largely went unnoticed and was generally undervalued. For all intents and purposes, this section of the operation was excellent.

I have fond memories of the staff, including Elwyn Walters (team manager; former Norths Brisbane, South Sydney, Eastern suburbs NSWRL and Australian Test player), a true gentleman and legend of the sport who made a huge impression on me. Another was Phil Economidis, a great servant of the game for whom I have much respect. He would later become the club's head coach.

## Communication Breakdown

*"Players had no interest in the machinations of the board. But we were aware of how relationships between board, CEO and coach could impact the organisation and, ultimately, our performance, which can be understated. This is dependent on the nature of the issue, fallout or breakdown of relationships."* *(Ray Herring, former captain Gold Coast Seagulls)*

Sadly, communications had broken down between senior executives, head coach and general staff during my tenure. Many of our issues were ignored, which created a feeling of negativity, while a gradual decline in communication led to many issues between the organisation, staff and athletes.

If these issues, conflicts and internal staff challenges had been addressed in an open manner to align with performance outcomes, many concerns would have been allayed. It was unfortunate that our issues were left unattended, which only frustrated everyone to a point of split alliances and "no return."

The significance of effective communication and leadership in this case provides context. It is sad that the indicators of poor results can be traced to an environment where views, opinions and expertise were ignored purely out of a neglect for a systematic approach to communication (e.g., regular meetings to address performance concerns). Proactive communication enables performance.

- Process Clarity

For example, I felt that we managed selection debates poorly when our coaching philosophies clashed. The lack of formal process was the catalyst for many of these debates while neglect of open communication led to further staff challenges.

This issue started very early in our preparation as squads were graded and separated. Although the grading process is required, I believe that managing the more talented and experienced players requires respect and an acknowledgement of the challenge of reclaiming their ranking in the squad. This is taken on a case-by-case basis, and dealing with both amateur and professional levels requires attention and respect from the coaching staff.

Managing this process required direct feedback to the athlete to outline areas for individual development and correction. An athlete's perception of staff treatment is an important key to their willingness to accept and work with these challenges. As a staffing body I felt we neglected the psychology of dealing with disgruntled athletes. Managing their ego can be readily offset by simply paying attention to their needs and providing appropriate feedback for their development.

From my perspective, the senior coach should manage this process and offer the necessary corrective and remedial detail to map players' progress back to top ranking.

My role as assistant coach was to enable this process, not manage it. There is a difference. As an assistant coach, discussing the players' path back to the first team without the senior coach's feedback is flawed. If the senior head coach was providing corrective feedback to the players, I was not aware. I largely managed this process unsupported, providing feedback to those players who approached me. I struggled with this situation, which suggests a defective structure of staff responsibility.

- Selection

Squad selections can take various forms, but generally all coaching staff are represented during this process. In our case, John Harvey, the senior head coach (former Manly, Eastern Suburbs professional player and later Salford, UK head coach), selected both squads, which ultimately devalued my contribution and role in the structure.

As previously stated, coaching staff must act collaboratively to develop stability and consistency of operation, even though conflict is inevitable. Debate is conducive to finding the best solution if the process is underpinned with honesty and transparency.

For example, communication between staff was all but non-existent to a point where I was questioning my role as a professional coach. Ad hoc changes would be made by the senior coach during the game without consultation. There is an obvious responsibility to both the staff and athlete that accompanies being the senior coach, including appropriate communication, planning and amendments to programs. In this case, notwithstanding the process being structurally flawed, the senior coach demonstrated a lack of formal process and respect for staff and, indirectly, the squad.

- Structure

Well-thought-out staffing models can be as simplistic or as complex as desired, but not at the expense of efficiency, effectiveness or purpose. An area I felt was missing in our leadership modelling was a framework whereby performance feedback functioned in a fashion that promoted purpose and intent to succeed. Success at elite levels demands coaching staff that are aligned in philosophy and performance is underpinned by consistency, fairness and a targeted purpose.

Our operating model was constantly challenged by staff because the lack of collective purpose became more evident as the year progressed and the organisation drifted apart.

As a result, I gradually became surplus to the structure, while others were being utilised in roles that were clearly part of my job description. Consequently, this avoidance and refusal to address philosophical differences created irreversible factions across the organisation, leading to a fractured environment that was consumed with innuendo and assertions.

- Confusion

Aside from the lack of a formal system of communication, there was absolutely no staff feedback, which further highlights the depth of concerns for employee and structure. An active, vibrant and aligned model provides staff and athlete an opportunity to grow as a matter of systematic feedback. An employee has a right to know what your expectations are through both remit and function. Through appropriate performance reviews, we are reminded of the specific deliverables of our role. This is a common business practice and the basis for employee–manager development, but it was non-existent during my tenure at Gold Coast.

To this day, I do not understand why my role altered, how my relationship with the senior head coach soured or what area of my work practice was in conflict. This situation was never discussed, and as a young, aspiring coach it was challenging and created self-doubt.

Perhaps I challenged the structure, systems and processes of the establishment, which may have in turn upset the status quo. Some perceived this as undermining the head coach, which may have split the organisation. Again, this was evidence of our inability to communicate or our fortitude to improve.

The club also missed an active senior playing group, which only exacerbated many of the coaching and performance concerns. I must add that there were experienced athletes in the playing group who would have benefited from a formal role as a senior player. An opportunity lost.

- Worth

By the competitive season's end, I was not in the organisation's planning. I am unclear what process my employer went through to arrive at their conclusions, but I was terminated without any explanation.

I felt completely betrayed by the lack of a system or executive support. As a young, developing coach, many questions consumed my thinking. Was it my work ethic? Was it my manner? Did I not work as a team member? Was I disrespectful? None of these questions were answered and, naturally, I struggled with the CEO's decision.

I was, however, privy to adverse behaviour and the outward rejection of my input or engagement with staff. Other staff were obviously seeking to disassociate from me for fear of reprisal. Not a nice feeling when you see "mates" become alienated due to perceived alliances.

Although conflict may lead to relationship fallouts, I was shocked to see how staff acted once they knew of my impending sacking. Betrayal caught me out twice in my career. Trust, loyalty and mateship count for nought if the dividend is high enough.

The tenure on the Gold Coast was a "time to grow up" moment in my career.

## Lessons

There were many lessons, including recognising an incoherent structure, acknowledging and learning how to deal with conflict, and detecting the warning signs.

Success, competitiveness and achievement based on honest and respectful collaboration are fundamental to any business model let alone in a high-performance setting. My belief in this instance is built on transparency while excellence is accompanied by clarity and integrity to attain consistency of performance.

Out of the carnage of this tenure, I assessed my role and tried to improve. Sitting atop my assessment was the validation for staying honest with players and staff. I value honesty and communicating with respect and attention to an athlete's goals. In fact, it is paramount to success and the realisation of the potential of the coach-athlete relationship.

Personalities and character obviously play a big part in all workplaces, but certainly the lack of a strong culture accounted for many of our issues. As part of the staff, I regret what happened at the Gold Coast club, but I will not apologise for my sincerity and honesty or the quality I demanded of my work for the athletes' benefit. I have never been challenged on my work ethic or how I support individual learning and development, which I still espouse today.

My coaching career is built on a platform of directness and transparency, occasionally at the expense of the individual's feelings. This is an area I have worked hard at, including undertaking studies in counselling psychology, which has helped immensely in my career.

- Trust

As a coach, building trust between staff and athletes is critical to making fair and consistent decisions, and it certainly assists team performance. This can be a difficult principle to live by in a professional sports environment where selections, respect and integrity can often be compromised for the sake of winning. Finding the balance will continually challenge your character as a coach, but to sacrifice your values to gain an edge for short-term benefit could lead to personal conflicts and create self-doubt in the squad.

Trust is fundamental in team sports, including in the player-coach relationship, which sits atop my priorities as a coach. If you cannot build trust with the athlete, performance and learning will be compromised to the detriment of the team.

## Our Role

Our role as coach is also to provide well-being and emotional support as the players fumble through life's challenges. The world of professionalism in team sport is littered with stories of conflict between staff, athletes and executives largely because we all live by varying standards and beliefs. As coach we hold an important position and must strive to build a safe and stable environment.

To undermine integrity and honesty in a team sense will challenge even the best to regain the confidence of the group. There is no room for the smoke-and-mirrors approach to gain an advantage over the athlete or the squad. The method is short-lived and, as a strategy, its worth is negligible!

I highly value respect and care in how I deal with those in my charge, but I have found that this can often be misconstrued as favouritism if those around you are not privy to what defines you personally within your role or how you are to function within the job. The level at which you operate is only as good or bad as the relationship built between the coach and athlete. The same applies to the influence on the athlete in their life. "Honesty is key. Tell me to my face what you think. Don't sugar-coat it. Being told how to fix my performance was critical, while feedback and communication are vital." Ray Herring (former Broncos and Gold Coast professional rugby league player)

The enormity of our role as coach is best described by the defined model of that relationship. Naturally, athletes (and staff) gravitate toward a person who outwardly displays or builds this connection. The illustration depicts the adverse reaction (i.e., the athlete detaching when integrity and trust are questioned).

Simply put, being honest can be a challenge for those around you if the management structure is not geared toward engaging and enabling staff. The flaw inside our model at Gold Coast started with the lack of clarity and communication and led to assertion and disharmony across various areas (e.g., selection policy).

Another area where we failed was managing the demands of professional coaching. "Doing it alone" is too big a responsibility in elite sport. Confidence and trust in your staff enable delegation and shared portfolios, which are commonplace to meet high-performance coaching demands (e.g., operations, coaching, media, academy and analysis should be shared).

The workload at this level is immense and all staff must play a role to cover it without fear of reprisal.

- Confront the Problem

The test of leadership, as I learnt, is to stay strong in your convictions and act only within those boundaries, without peer influence. This is easier said than done if you are in a subordinate role.

At the elite level of sport there is no room for hiding from issues or delaying when to address those concerns. When confronted with a losing culture, substandard performances or staff disharmony, the time to act and remain true to your convictions is now! The consequences of not dealing with problems as they arise are a dysfunctional operation.

As a young and immature coach, I was often overawed by the magnitude of these decisions we were making that greatly affect the athletes' futures. We must be cognisant of the process in which we engage and the reaction or consequences of those decisions. Overseeing these decisions carries a responsibility to not only the club and stakeholders, but also the individual. You should be clear and concise when dealing with selection issues and always allow the athlete to manage his journey back to top form while you act as the support.

Accordingly, issues that arise between staff members generally take time to reach a point of open conflict (i.e., argument). If the situation is ignored, no one benefits, and the environment will become toxic and infect all facets of the operation. As a coach, effective leadership includes having strong conversations and confronting those debates that affect the players' environment and their performance. Ignoring the problems will result in poor relationships between coaches and athletes.

Because of our inability to confront issues at Gold Coast, the performance of staff and players suffered while relationships were challenged and fractured.

- Show Your Personality

Trust is central as the mentor, confidant and leader. These are all important facets of being the coach and the characteristics the player is looking for in their coach. Being in charge holds a far greater function (i.e., to serve and support), while trust defines coaching.

At times during this period, my instinct to support the player had been kept in check so as not to upset the management and the perception of who was in charge. In the end, I continued to work with those players who came to me for advice, regardless of the consequences. This is considered normal practice where all coaching staff are enabled to function as a part of a system. Insecurity and fear drove coaches to hinder and stifle my contribution while many players feared reprisal if they sought my advice — sad. Coming to me was also seen as showing your allegiance (i.e., between head coach and assistant coach)! Factions had developed.

Perhaps that contributed to me losing my job?

Working in an environment where you conceal your personality is untenable and will ultimately affect your development and the performance of those around you. A fear of revealing who you are and what defines you as a person and as a coach will generally lead to conflict.

To avoid conflict at the Gold Coast, I was more inclined to conceal my character and philosophy to ensure that there was calm between the staff members. To a point, I hid my intellect, my game knowledge and my management skill to appease the inadequacy of our structure and management.

Due to my immaturity and inexperience, I avoided the issues that contributed to the demise of various relationships within the management team. Was this my job? I think everyone has a responsibility to speak up and highlight concerns irrespective of position or the potential fallout! I didn't speak out. I should have gone to the CEO, but I feared losing my job, which turned out to be the case anyway.

## Dealing with Failure

If the operation is built on honesty, it will avoid many issues. As was the case at my Gold Coast tenure, mistakes were a result of poor decision making, poor management, unclear communication and not confronting problems.

As a staff, we badly failed the players, club and supporters. Dealing with organisational differences was neglected and, as a result, poor performance, disharmony and conflict occurred. Strong, engaging and supportive leadership is fundamental to success in managing conflict, but how you apply the characteristics of leadership in the context of your personality is key. If you disguise your character, the integrity of your role will come into question. Be honest with yourself and those around you.

**Postscript by Kevin Campion** (former Ireland international; Queensland State of Origin and NRL premiership winning player)

*This period at the Gold Coast Seagulls (1992-1995) was the best and most difficult period of my career. I met some great characters who are still mates today. Sadly, it was an unstable environment borne out of poor culture and "indifferent" leadership style from coaches and senior players.*

*Personally, it was a case of "if you don't know, you just don't know." It wasn't until playing at other clubs that I realised how poorly managed Gold Coast Seagulls was. There was a culture of every man for himself; it wasn't "we," it was definitely "me."*

*There was no expectation; we were so used to losing that it became a habit. There was a lack of direction, and players were intimidated, not enabled. They were too proud to ask for assistance. We were functioning blindly. You can't build a culture on a foundation like that.*

# CHAPTER 7

# Loyalty, Trust and Integrity

Over many years I have learnt that alignment between vision and performance is an ideal state, particularly when observing the multifaceted challenges that exist between coaching staff, players and the organisation. Pursuing alignment can also be confusing and misguided when discussing the personality, values and integrity of the organisation. The gaps are immeasurable in some cases and in other ways a contradiction of sorts.

Conflict and the need for direction between the board's expectations and (realistic) goals set by the organisation is one of the challenges mentioned in this chapter. This will always be a constant discussion; alignment continually shifts, and staff constantly collide on views, opinions and perceptions of direction. These collisions may have a positive or negative impact on alignment depending on the context of those discussions, which include the consequences to performance and shifting of goals.

There are many facets to coaching, including the constant search for alignment of goals and philosophies. I have found that using goals will provide your athletes and staff with a sense of holistic worth and motivation for success. Therefore, alignment may be best served by having those discussions knowing this to be an ideal and not a requirement to achieving success.

Standards, honour and trustworthiness are more important to me when discussing the core of the business and the drive for success. If alignment is to be achieved, it must start with the hired help and an intent to discuss company direction as a phase of development rather than promoting a desired state of success that will rarely be achieved.

## Background

While in the UK during the Rugby League World Cup (2000), I was approached by Leeds Rhinos Rugby to fill a supporting role (technical director) in what was a very difficult time for the club — more so off the field, as I was to learn. At the time, I was still under contract with Melbourne Storm, but I was granted a release. It was difficult leaving Melbourne, but the opportunity to work in a new environment was an exciting prospect that would further my development.

Professionally, I needed a fresh start and the Leeds offer was a timely opportunity and one not to miss, especially considering the high esteem in which the club was held. I also knew Head Coach Dean Lance (former Western Reds; Adelaide Rams head coach; former professional Canberra Raider, Grand Final winner) and some of the players, which influenced my decision.

In no way are these accounts meant to recreate actual events; I have merely used recollections of specific occurrences as a backdrop to explain situations that challenge our roles as coaches. Professionally, this event also provided another check to the harsh reality of professional coaching. At the time, any sense of alignment would have been welcomed by the club.

## Part 1 - Setting the Scene

The style of the English game was refreshing compared with the Australian game. Defence was secondary, while the attack, support and free-flowing ball movement provided another element where I could develop. The attacking skill set of the players was excellent. Each team had several standout players who could have transitioned to the NRL, which has been proven many times since.

Fitness levels were adequate and applied sports science was still in its infancy at the time. Discussing these differences between the English and Australian game was a subject to handle with care. It was a very sensitive subject for both players and staff, as I learnt. Speaking honestly was not going to win me any friends; I became guarded because of their reaction when I spoke too directly. Finding the correct method of communication without reprisal challenged me for many years while coaching in England and later in Scotland and Ireland.

The English game was entertaining, highlighted by an open style of play that appealed to television audiences and the fans. There was an importance to winning the Challenge Cup while the Super League final series was a relatively new innovation and secondary in their quest for silverware. The Challenge Cup has a long history in the game; it is revered and the ultimate achievement in the UK game. My understanding at the time, although naive, was more about surviving the promotion and relegation that was still in vogue in the Super League.

As technical director, I reported on the club's status and went about highlighting planning relevant to achieving a stable, functioning elite environment for the players. The extract below (board report - June 2001) shows my findings and appropriate changes, while many of my recommendations were not implemented due to various changes that would be made at the club.

Concerns:

- Lack of planning has presented several problems with the internal running of the football department including the absence of "common goals" that can be driven from section to section.

- Many staff possess individual philosophies on work-related issues, which presents obvious problems within the framework of the organisation.
- Structurally, the sections operate independently, which causes overlapping and time wastage when addressing everyday problems.
- Retrieval of documentation (i.e., minutes, reports and such) is a major concern in terms of planning, delegation and assessment of "corrective action."
- Interviewing of staff resulted in concern due to the lack of feedback on their roles and performances.

Note: With the introduction of a strategic plan and the implementation of departmental section plans, control and stability to operational procedures will alleviate the broad-based concerns outlined above.

As a progressive club, Leeds was chasing the secrets to value-add that drive success. From my initial observations, there was an existing depth of players and experienced and innovative staff, while the executive had a long-term view to achieve sustainable success. All the ingredients were there, including a well-resourced operation. At the time, it was obvious that the club's academy was riddled with gifted players who would provide a platform to the club's success for many years.

Unfortunately, the issues that hampered their quest for silverware were not on the field but off. The team was good enough, but performance was sidelined by an internal conflict.

**Part 2 – Setting the Scene**

On arrival, it was apparent there was a rift between the club, head coach (Dean Lance), and a leading player (Paul Sterling) over a racism claim as a catalyst for non-selection. The player had escalated the complaint to a court hearing that could have been damaging to his and the coach's career. The head coach defended his integrity and profession largely independently from the club. Because of this issue, the club and staff struggled to win back the confidence of the squad as the circumstances created inevitable factions. Over the ensuing months, staff worked tirelessly to unite the club. However, the personal nature of this situation meant that it ended badly for the coach.

## Honesty

It became apparent that irrespective of a coach's qualities, their integrity is constantly being judged. The head coach had proven himself in professional appointments many times. It is sad that his credibility and character had been questioned and it ultimately cost the coach his job. During this challenging period, Dean never stopped displaying integrity and resilience, and he would not be compromised. He never questioned his moral sense and was strong under pressure. No matter how convincing the argument, I have struggled with this case and the brutality of this side of professional sport.

As a close observer, there seemed to be only minimal involvement by club executive, which demonstrated an inability to mediate internally, provide public clarity or show a sense of care or respect for those involved. I am sure the club provided an appropriate level of support behind the scenes, but it appeared that the situation required a stance derived from its own internal investigation and organisational ethics. This would have served the club's integrity well.

The loneliness of elite coaching was becoming all too apparent, as I watched conflicted players and staff contemplate their loyalty. It was sad that others (i.e., friends, family and staff) become involved either indirectly being associated or as a direct relationship. For me, this was another déjà vu feeling from previous experiences of being alienated with the Gold Coast Seagulls. It was a feeling I was becoming familiar with.

As pressure mounted on the head coach, factions were borne that left alignment a world away.

## Conflicted

Loyalty and betrayal meet us all at some point in our careers while compromise may have its short-lived reward. There are times when we may become conflicted with this option and the choice or appeal of an "easy route" challenges our sense of value.

I was tested on my interest for the head coach position by a senior member of the organisation. Having observed the demise of the previous coach, friend and mentor, I could have been forgiven for my lack of interest in the position. It was an example of compromised trust with little regard for loyalty. Once again, memories of my previous experiences flooded back as the coaching role became vacant. I fully accept that the order of business needed to return, and the club needed a coach ASAP.

To align and pull the club back together required a systematic approach to manage the fallout and to provide clarity of the operation for the future. What I observed was a need to find a quick replacement to restore order. Maybe the organisation had a contingency plan. The incumbent head coach was found on staff and for all intents and purposes he may have just fallen into the role.

What changed was my role with the new coach, which was always going to make this appointment difficult. When a coach is replaced, the incumbent generally inherits the system and structures. In this case, a group of players loyal to the previous coach presented issues for the incumbent.

My role during this period was to provide transitional support for the incumbent — a difficult assignment considering my friendship with Dean and the incumbent winning the position from a less than transparent process that upset some sections of the playing staff who had built a strong relationship with the outgoing coach. This is a reality of professional coaching.

When trust, loyalty and honesty are compromised, players will challenge the "how and why" of what is happening around them. Invariably, acting without integrity catches up as I witnessed the conflicted reactions and emotions of senior executives, players and staff when the head coach was sacked. Athletes appreciate fairness and routine, and our athletes in Leeds had been disrupted — unfairly, it seemed.

## Lessons

Leeds Rugby is one of the most successful UK clubs of the modern era, having built a strong academy, a reputation for astute player signings and a team that coaches want to coach. The club demands respect, and winning trophies is its goal.

- Ruthless

Professional sport requires an unobstructed vision, like-minded brokers and a strong constitution for dealing with conflict. Leeds Rugby was all that and more, but the cost to personal welfare was secondary to winning. Being privy to the demise of their head coach and how management, supporters and players were divided provided an up close and personal look at the fragility of professional sports and the effects on people's lives.

- Success and the Greater Good

My time at Leeds provided an invaluable lesson about honour, integrity and respect and where they fit within the scope of coaching. Professionally speaking, honour as a characteristic of your coaching sells a clear message to your team and staff where comradery and collegial actions exist. Honour leads to a genuine respect for people and how we operate, while integrity underpins how we exist in a professional setting. These characteristics of operations also bind the team and staff and guide their actions and performance.

At Leeds, management were experienced but we sacrificed our values to a point during a challenging time. Team performance cannot survive without trust and confidence inside the management, staff and playing group. There is obvious benefit where trust, teamwork and harmony has been built in a manner that promotes a sense of self-belief and morale.

Sport typically takes no prisoners and losing is unforgivable — a hard marker in a two-horse race. Understanding the expectations of professional coaching can offset many of the dramas that inevitably unfold, but no matter how long or how successful you are as a coach, you will be judged!

As a leader in professional sport, you need to make decisions that sit well with the fans and are media friendly. Critical decisions, such as removing a coach, are made for many reasons, largely borne out of losing or an untenable relationship. In some instances, sacking a coach can be perceived as unprofessional and lacking integrity and respect for the person and family. This course of action (sacking) is situational as reflected in my time at Leeds, which demonstrates a potential conflict between moral conviction and organisational objectives.

What I witnessed at Leeds was arguably at the expense of the individual's credibility and professional standing. Being replaced is part of the landscape of professional coaching (and playing), and I accept that credibility or experience is irrelevant if the situation is untenable. As coaches we realise that our roles are performance-driven; but this does not disqualify organisations from being accountable and transparent in difficult periods when staff face challenging periods.

- In the "Best Interests" of the Club

It's sad that a coach's fate is often driven by media and fans, which can ultimately affect family, career and other players. Unfortunately, players often become the meat in the sandwich — but, generally, agents protect their contracts and side with the club's decision. As a coach, you can be rest assured that players will bend with the media slant, while agents generally support the athletes' decision.

I quickly learnt to be of strong character with the knowledge that players, fans and the media ultimately decide my fate. I know very few coaches who remain unscathed during their careers; all coaches will feel the pain of being sacked at some time.

## Performance is Paramount

Lose often enough and you will be sacked. Winning is a commodity which is utilised in various manners, such as player trades and generating income through sponsors, investors and stakeholders. The real issue for the coach is the win–loss ratio, business and player squad development, and public perception. Manage these defining elements and your tenure will generally last the term of the contract. This is by no means an easy feat! For most, the start of a professional coaching tenure is the beginning of the end!

Coaching is a learnt skill and along the way you gain experience, sport-specific intelligence and leadership qualities, all of which will be tested with varying degrees of success and failure. Remember that not all environments will suit your methods, philosophy or perceptions. Being sacked does not mean you are a poor coach. Character, methodology and relationships feature heavily when evaluating the effectiveness of the coach.

In coaching, successful outcomes contribute the most to determining how effective the coach is, while peripheral elements such as media, spectators and stakeholders will also play a part in determining a coach's future. Your tenure is largely out of your control and often at the bequest of others in the system.

# CHAPTER 8

# Professionalism

So, what does it mean to be truly professional? There are many questions that complicate my response, but at times professionalism is an illusion borne from inappropriate or irrelevant behaviour and actions. Let me explain.

The standard and quality of my workplace is defined by work ethic, attention to detail and the values by which the business operates. Being committed and dedicated to the task is how you perform and should naturally underpin being professional without being tasked.

Excellence is often used to describe professionalism, though I am more inclined to discuss performance or those actions that enable professionalism. For the most part, being "professional" is self-driven and should be effortless. In a professional sense, attitude provides your view of excellence.

I am always refining my approach to how I lead. I am continually evaluating my communication and people management techniques to refine and enhance functionality. All coaching decisions should be made with the athlete's environment and development in mind.

The following references are from a time when I had over a decade of professional coaching experience at an elite level. I had experienced the highs and lows, including being part of a winning environment and, conversely, being sacked. By the time I had reached this stage of my career, the concept of professionalism had become more confusing than ever. Little wonder I lacked a sense of clarity around the expectations of what it is to be a professional coach!

One area that created confusion was the conflict between my perception of being a professional and the standards of those around me. Differing standards, values and work ethics are a part of all work environments. The more I understood those attitudinal differences, the more I realised how to manage my actions, behaviour and professional standards, although this experience failed to support my role in the following account.

## Setting

The account I have provided in this chapter offers examples of when I was conflicted on several levels as a high-performance coach. It was a time when I questioned my sense of self-worth, and my value and integrity were challenged.

My expectations of the business were clear in terms of winning. But when the how, why and what were challenged during tough periods, senior executives struggled to maintain their sincerity or respect for our agreed (club) vision.

These events transpired during my tenure as head coach of Warrington (UK Super League). Our operation appeared to be functional at one level but, when challenged, conflicted at another level. The detail of the various day-to-day management tasks across recruitment, coaching and performance expectations would be considered typical inside the workings of an elite rugby organisation today. However, I found an organisation misfiring when leadership was required to manage organisational conflict in an orderly and professional manner. Crucial operational concerns were out of reach of our management team, leading to overly ambitious performance expectations and business goals.

## Background

My time at Warrington was an exciting but turbulent period. I came to the club as an experienced coach and left confused, battered and bruised, largely from poor decisions I made. I still feel fortunate to have coached at such an historic club. Sadly, history and tradition do not always equate to professionalism or success, as I was to find out. Warrington was another challenging appointment.

The club had an interesting structure, with a CEO who had limited rugby experience and a lord as chairman. Only in England! While knowledge of rugby was not essential for the CEO, a greater understanding of the game could have better served the organisation. Although they were supportive to a point, I looked to other qualified people to assist in matters of specifics, which appeared to be my only alternative at the time.

The board was supportive and listened intently to any issues I presented when we met. Generally, I would see the chairman on game day, and I would soon learn that my immediate staff were my sole support. Out of necessity, I sought advice from England head coach and personal friend, David Waite.

We were based at a college campus and used classrooms and fields, while the gym was a mixed arrangement between a local fitness centre and school-based equipment. It was inadequate for a professional team.

I brought one staff member (David Plange, former Hunslet and Leeds Rhinos academy head coach) to Warrington and inherited the previous regime's coaches. All had passion but possessed only minimal senior coaching experience. The staff and facility lacked structural resources and experience as we struggled to recruit marquee players, which was not ideal considering we were playing in top-flight competition!

# Leadership

Poor decisions that lacked the maturity required for a head coach were the mark of my tenure. Those poor decisions were exposed as I grappled with issues that were outside my head coaching remit! I learnt to control the controllable and focus on events that worked in my favour. At Warrington I lost my way and had taken my eyes off the ball as challenges mounted around me. Too many operational concerns, such as budgets and facility issues, consumed my day. These are clearly important for a high-performance program, but they are not part of my role!

As the season passed, eventually my focus turned to those issues that I felt were directly impacting squad performance. It was too little too late.

- Financial Position

My starting point was a simple request: asking for all player contracts and the budget. Executive presented several budgets before I received anywhere near the facts. I could not get one budget that told me exactly where the club was financially positioned, let alone a spreadsheet with the relevant player contract values. I was operating in the dark.

If Warrington had been honest about its financial situation, I would not have taken the position. Maybe other applicants for the job were privy to this. I certainly was not, and I was continually thrown decoys when I requested financials. The operating budget is key for any planning, particularly for player recruitment and retention, which I also managed. I was never clear on player budgets.

- A Big Mistake

My greatest blunder was opening my coaching theories to the media. I presented an outline to the club executives and the media. My plan was based around building the academy program, retaining local talent and not selling them off to other clubs, which is a generally accepted process in pro sport in Europe. I honestly outlined that the plan needed time to mature. I was confident we would survive relegation and with patience could enjoy long-term success. It was quite sad when my plan was used by the media to undo my vision.

The extract below (Part 8 — Targets) sat alongside academy and development plans and worked on a simple theory of (1) making the base strong to enable stability (2) before reaching a series of outcomes. (3) Planning included a review process and (4) resetting targets.

| Basement (1) | Stability (2) | Outcome (3) |
| --- | --- | --- |
| Introducing culture and coaching ethos | Setting higher expectations and standards | Raising the bar on team performance |
| Individual focus on preparation and standards | Increase demands on team performance | Determine concrete team outcomes and results |
| Assessment of playing personnel to improve standards | Continue to develop player potential at the base | Increase expectations and outcomes on all junior programs |
| Youth policy introduced | Squad predominately Under-21 | Consistent recruitment and retention |
| Debuting of young talent | Introduce our programs to selected feeder clubs | Secured feeder club system |
| Target: 50-55% wins | Target: 60-65% wins | Target: 70-75% wins |

Coaching can be a lonely place at times, and this was my first real taste of it. I remember this time well as the team struggled for wins and lost support while supporters were frantic and the media hyped up the situation to ensure that one story fed another. I was not panicking, but it was unfortunate for me that the club executives quickly lost sight of the long-term approach, which was the beginning of the end for me.

## Recruitment

We had a strong international contingent at the club, including professionals from France, Wales, New Zealand, Australia and Papua New Guinea. This trend continued due to the lack of local product as I recruited players to improve the quality and depth of the squad.

During this period, I also presented a plan that ensured local talent was retained. Succession planning is paramount to recruitment while the academy program should provide the long-term support needed for building the talent pool to ensure depth and consistency of performance. It is sad that much of this process had been neglected at Warrington in favour of a quick fix approach to recruitment: buying quality players. In the long term, this is cost inefficient and does little to retain local talent.

- Team Performance

When I commenced duties, I took the time to observe and not change too much. This was an opportunity to watch players perform, train and interact with one another, which are all crucial elements for building a team. However, we placed all players on notice at the start of my tenure, which seemed to get a rise out of the group as we went about tidying up areas of the program that needed it. Performances were at best inconsistent while the talent in the squad was aging. This squad had been put together with short-term gain in mind, which was reflected in a lack of investment in their academy structure. This was an area of focus in my early work at the club.

At the backend of the initial season (2001) we had played quite well, finishing a credible seventh in the final standings. There was some indifferent form during this period, and we competed well with top clubs but lost to the less fancied teams. Obviously, that was an issue and one area that I hoped to address as part of the ensuing season's preparation. This included the redesign of our resources program and increasing functional and intensity training performance outcomes. The following season started well with a series of steady performances, including a Challenge Cup qualifying victory and a season opening win.

- Juggling Act

A test of character for the club, the squad and me as head coach began to unravel. Many of these challenges came about through inconsistent performance and losing. As a professional coach, finding the balance between long-term planning, club, stakeholder, and board expectations, and winning is key. At another level there were issues surrounding acceptance of the change of style I had ushered in, with many of the squad failing to transition and adapt. This is not unusual as methodology and changes of coaching method are made and players must adapt. My style of developing a philosophy is built around long-term objectives while striving for short-term gains in consistency and performance.

Culturally, there was also an undercurrent between the home nation players and the overseas contingent, borne out of perceived bias between salaries. It was sad that what the imports brought to the organisation was overlooked (i.e., elite experience, aligned expectations, leadership) and they often became scapegoats for losing performances.

My greatest hurdle during this period was convincing many of the players that "structured play" was necessary to develop "unstructured" styles. Unfortunately, we did not have the depth of firepower and a systems approach was new to many of the players. Although we lacked firepower in certain positions, we did not achieve any noticeable change or adaptation to my systems. Either way, not achieving results nor players adapting to a style of game is a failure on any level as a professional coach.

- Media

Indifferent performance generally opens the door to media speculation, often lacking substance or context. It was concerning at many levels.

My relationship with the media was strained. I did what was expected of me, but at the same time I would not bow to their attitude or demands, the drummed-up hype or unconstructive commentary about our performances. Most of these reports were designed to spark a reaction from me, which I could have managed better so the media and supporters were kept informed. In a way I was controlling our media using scripted releases, but I should have played a greater role in supporting information "in and out" of the club to our advantage.

In hindsight, I should have ignored the local media's campaign that had rooted from a disdain toward my proposed five-year plan. The media, not the club, wanted immediate results that, realistically, wouldn't be attained for several years. Some of the reporting was, at best, ordinary and fuelled the campaign to terminate the program.

From what I had observed, planning had played only a minor part in the club's previous coaching campaigns. This is not an attack on those who preceded my appointment nor their programs, for that matter. This statement is an observation made of those in senior executive roles at the time who had accepted my program but deserted my work when the media drove its agenda to dislodge me and my plan.

The brief (extract) below is taken from a report by England head coach David Waite (former head coach Newcastle Nights and St. George Dragons) who was seconded to conduct an internal review of my operation. It was sad that this report was lost in translation by the media and, obviously, Warrington's board! However, it is some validation of my program by a respected coach.

Warrington Brief

*"Obviously very interesting to observe firsthand your management style. You appear, on all fronts, to have come a long way in a short time frame with your `influence` in Warrington. What a surprise!! I can only hope that those in charge are prepared to see your planning through as I believe this is*

*Warrington's best phase, for a long time, to push toward the desired goal (i.e., year in and year out consistent improvement not only in performance on the park but through the full 360 that senior Super League clubs need to work in). To be consistently in the top 6 is no doubt one of all club's goals. You know better than I do what is possible in the finals competition."*

The media played a large part in complicating my tenure at Warrington. It was borne out of the innuendo of a few persons connected in the "right places" who were privy to specific aspects of my planning. As far as transparency goes, I openly presented my program to the media and had the board's consent. The board had agreed we needed a long-term vision that promoted sustainability based around building success on the back of the academy product. This contrasted with the practice of the organisation buying overseas players and paying above the odds for their services. I supported the adage of reinvesting in the academy.

As the challenges mounted, I gradually lost respect for the media and was disgusted by how the club's issues were played out in the public domain. It was devastating and affected the squad's morale. Inadvertently, the local paper became judge, jury and executioner as it incited supporters to rally for change of coach as the team battled for traction. Poor media management contributed to an unstable environment, which resulted in the club appointing several head coaches during a very short period around my tenure. I am not sure where the responsibility lays.

As an example of the media's disdain for my processes, I had decided to play a young player (prop, Paul Wood) and set about to protect him from issues that may add to his pressure. To assist him I placed a media ban around him to ease the pressure and because he was inexperienced in handling the media. This was about protecting the player with consideration of his maturity and the enormity of the event for him. I would do the same again to protect him.

The fallout over the media ban was a disgrace, including a suggestion to ban all forms of media for that game. That did not happen, but the post-match conference was not a nice place to be. I was still furious that protecting a young player in such an important week of his career was totally misconstrued. I was later accused of interfering in the media's right to interview players, which was never the case. My action to shelter the player from pressure was not unique, and it was considered in the context of the player's youth and inexperience.

- Demise

After suffering five straight defeats I received an urgent request to attend a board meeting to discuss "where to go from here." None of these losses were by large margins as we lost games in crucial moments through poor decisions. This was not unusual for a squad of young players. The squad needed time to gel as new combinations, squad confidence and playing style developed under new structures.

I reiterated the significance of patience and having confidence in the squad and staff. The board was worried about criticism and the flak from the local media. It was also concerned about the sponsors. At this moment, I knew that all that I had presented, constructed and implemented was in jeopardy. I decided to step down as head coach and assume my primary role of performance director.

My role as coach had been undermined by a lack of support from several factions, but none more so than by the board and the media. The media drummed-up support to replace me with a local hero, which I believe had been the essence of the undertone prior to my appointment — one will never know. The board never denied those rumours that ultimately resurfaced. The power of the media was used to manoeuvre and manipulate while the character of the club's powerbrokers wavered.

This was a time in my career when I started to second-guess my philosophies. When I eventually left the club some six weeks after stepping down as head coach, the brutality of professional coaching hit home as I attempted to deconstruct events. I feel I demonstrated a sense of commitment during my tenure while quitting became a last resort.

### Lessons

I must reiterate that these observations are merely accounts and interpretations from my role as the head coach. Any comments that may conflict with others' is a matter for conjecture and based on their opinions of the course of events.

This time in my career certainly challenged my thinking about people and how their roles within business may affect their values and beliefs. Those who hold crucial roles seem to be free of guilt or ownership for their part in not fulfilling expectations. When I arrived, the club was financially challenged, had limited investment in the academy and was operating without a long-term plan. The club did not provide a player roster that had depth or a plan built around succession. I asked questions about these matters at the time of my appointment and was met with indifferent responses from senior executives. This was a lesson learnt and a mistake I never made again. There were many awakenings that prepared me for far greater career challenges ahead. To say I was misinformed by senior executives would be harsh. I didn't ask the right questions.

## Trial by Media

I totally underestimated the power of the media. I learnt from this experience and realised that media perception can bring down a career. The media certainly influenced my decision to step down, as the team was bombarded with adverse commentary on the back of indifferent performances. The pressure the media exerted triggered a series of events by the board that would see me isolated and offered up as a scapegoat. I felt let down professionally and personally and received no support to offset the media barrage.

When I accepted the role, I opened the door to the media to include, engage and build appropriate relations with the public. I advocate for working with the media to provide an insight into your planning, but if the information is not managed or a true reflection of your work, there will be consequences, including having it used against you.

The media can be helpful, but ensure that the relationship is built on an even playing field that is conducive to both parties. This did not happen as there was continual manipulation of information that serviced the media's perceived outcomes. In saying this, I also recognise I fell victim to my own hard-nosed approach to the media and my inability to waver or compromise for the greater good. Right or wrong, I acted in a forthright and principled — albeit flawed and imperfect — manner.

- Betrayal, People and Character

I learnt the harsh reality of boardroom politics and that personal agendas can compromise the essence of your program. I certainly found out how strong the club's convictions were when my team was struggling; I needed support. People will naturally bond over success while failure tends to drive people apart, and factions naturally occur. I did not expect total isolation from the board, which highlighted the inexperience of the club and stakeholders in handling adversity. No matter how many times I reiterated to the supporters via the media that this team was a development project and patience was needed, it fell on deaf ears.

Losing can bring out the worst in people and some end up betraying you in their actions and their silence. As I struggled to find answers that would improve team performance, I was further isolated while the board, management and players fractured under the pressure. I had few supporters during this period. Of course, when you win everyone becomes your friend.

Someone once said, "Those who don't know the value of loyalty can never appreciate the cost of betrayal," and I agree.

- Due Diligence

Do your due diligence when considering a contract offer! I quickly accepted the contract as head coach and dealt with the cards as they fell. My due diligence amounted to a discussion with the outgoing coach and contact with the governing body on the club's performance. I neglected the most important area in the organisation — the club's leaders and management philosophy! As a professional coach, due diligence must be your number one priority when contemplating a career move.

My negligence and lack of foresight, in part, cost me my role and that has bugged me for many years. Conversely, I had the respect of committed senior players who had also been privy to all aspects of my planning. The players were more committed to the cause than the board was, but the reality was that I had not gained the confidence, support or respect of those who had hired me.

I learnt an invaluable lesson: to be successful in your coaching environment, alignment of objectives, systems and philosophy is fundamental. I also found that organisational integrity, loyalty and/or respect for player and staff is as profound as simply winning week to week. They have minimal influence in the grand scheme of things. Could I have done more? Naturally, wounds heal with time and reflection led to questioning my performance in greater detail.

Arguably, I left the program in a healthier place than when I arrived. My academy plan, service area plan, rugby operation model and an affordable player list secured their position as a Super League squad. Unfortunately, the board and CEO's lack of support forced me to resign and invariably challenged the team's ability to perform. Do I own their poor showing? Yes, in part. But there were many decisions made by the board that were out of my control, including pressuring me to a point where I resigned.

My tenure at Warrington stung. I was an experienced career coach and now I was contemplating leaving the industry. It was a decision not taken lightly but one that suited my family, career and health. At this point, leaving Rugby League expedited a career change to Rugby Union that I had been considering for some time.

- Inexperience and Support

My naivety in dealing with boards, how they operate and where I should place my trust cost me dearly, and the effects overlapped into my function as coach. Instead of being focussed on the playing group, I became entrenched in the peripheral issues and the survival of my job. Professional coaching is a constant reminder of the frailties in people in how they perceive and operate under pressure. There is no greater educator than experience.

These tough times are when you need a confidant — someone who sits outside your immediate workplace but has the experience to draw upon and can provide an unbiased ear. Due to my inexperience, I tried to manage my way through the turmoil solo!

My experience at Warrington has made me much more attuned, aligned and decisive about people, jobs and organisational culture. Consequently, my inner circle of trusted companions has decreased considerably as I consciously consider their loyalties — an easy process and consideration when experience becomes your friend. The old adage of "There are some things you have to experience to understand," is very true.

- Change, Resourcing and Legacy

Firstly, I misjudged the strength of the club to cope with change. I had experienced an organisation that was under-resourced compared with other franchises, was functionally challenged and lacked a clearly defined vision. Certainly, if the board had a vision, it never let me into its thinking, although I was aware of their bid for a new stadium.

As a professional coach, you must decide where your role starts and finishes. I was side-tracked as I looked at ways to shore up the players' pathways. This is a task that usually rests with the general manager, a position which did not exist until I took it on. Trying to assist in areas outside my primary role of coaching was my first major mistake as a head coach. My role, although clear, conflicted with a structure that was under-manned and under-resourced. I attempted to fill those roles at the expense of my coaching remit.

My second mistake was overestimating the players' ability to learn new systems, even though the stepped changes were planned over three years. The players were fine with this approach of building a style of game readily recognisable as Warrington. My main struggle was getting the organisation's buy-in and an acknowledgement of an approach commensurate with elite rugby that was supported by long-term development initiatives.

Upon reflection, my program was "too much, too soon" for the players, staff and club. Building a winning culture and a sustainable and consistently performing club takes time, resourcing and patience with an awareness of the significant challenges that lay ahead. As I mentioned, my due diligence on the business and executive commitment was flawed, contributing to a plan built on unstable foundations.

At times I felt completely lost and unsupported while attempts to reinvigorate our environment were ignored. I was never supported nor did I win the favour of any directors. Did I give up? Due to the board's inability to support, lead or actively promote strategic intent, yes, I did.

- Staff

Select your own staff because inheriting staff will invariably affect performance. At elite levels of the game, you need strong and supportive staff who understand the demands and challenges of being in a professional setting. At Warrington, I felt that my inexperience influenced my decision to maintain current backroom staff, which was to the detriment of the players' and the team's performance.

I needed to implement a model with a top-to-bottom change, but due to financial restrictions, I was only able to make minor changes to the staffing and structure. After assessing the existing staff, I knew I had not been strong enough in standing by my proposed staffing model.

Support staff are critical to performance at the elite level. Your staffing model must be based on your coaching needs and, more importantly, have the experience to work independently as needed. I had no time to act as a mentor. I worked hard to shuffle the existing staff into my model, which was a mistake. None of the inherited staff members were experienced enough to assume these roles. They were all very good in their own way, but the level of detail and scope that I required was not achievable. I attempted to absorb the missing components. This was another major blunder in my tenure and compromised many facets of the role as the pressure increased.

**Postscript by Matt Rodwell** (former Warrington captain; former Penrith, Newcastle, St. George and Western Reds professional)

*As I read back through Steve's account of what was an incredibly challenging period for him, both personally and professionally, my admiration grows. Steve's ability to protect the playing group from the internal turmoil and his struggles with budget, facilities and management support are testament to his strong character and understanding of coaching.*

*As one of several Australian players on the squad, we recognised the facilities and club structure were below our previous experiences, but we all looked upon the situation as a unique opportunity to continue playing professionally. Steve supported this view by not once using the facilities (or lack thereof) nor his battles with management as an excuse or a barrier to success — we soldiered on and attempted to bring some of our Australian professionalism to the squad.*

*It's fair to say the quality and depth of the playing squad was never going to challenge for a finals position while several of the players failed to meet the professional expectations and standards asked for by the coach. Nonetheless, Steve remained disciplined and consistent in his coaching application.*

*With age comes maturity and deeper understanding of challenges we all face — with this hindsight, I feel somewhat guilty and disappointed with myself that as a playing group we failed in our support of Steve as coach and did not demand from management further support for Steve's program.*

*Steve has not received the recognition he deserves for his ability to manage through club management dysfunction and maintain his coaching focus and philosophy. No doubt, the 'Warrington experience' unjustly harmed his reputation as a head coach.*

*One only must look at Warrington in recent years with a new owner and finances to compete with the other Super League heavyweights, the positive impact on the playing group and on-field performance.*

# The Changing Coach Environment — Discussing the consequences of change and defining high performance

*This section on high-performance coaching in the current professional workplace could not have resonated better with my experiences. Too often the challenges of being a coach and the relationship with the executive, the ultimate decision-makers, are misunderstood. Steve accurately outlines this, and the many other issues young, aspiring coaches face in today's coaching world.*

*His thorough understanding of how a practical high-performance model works is the most realistic assessment I have ever read. Where others fall down the rabbit hole of pure rhetoric, Steve provides a practical and workable solution for a productive high-performance vision.*

- Gary Gold (USA Rugby head coach; former head coach London Irish UK; Western Province, SA, Sharks, Super Rugby; Newcastle, Bath and Worcester, UK Premiership)

Several personal examples from high-performance (HP) coaching roles that I have held provide a backdrop to the significance of culture, planning and executive commitment to secure change. What is crucial for change is governance support and an executive actively facilitating continuous improvement. Executive support is critical when discussing change.

I discuss change as a constant and a necessary element of professional coaching to keep pace with competitors. Change as a process of review is also presented to challenge the boundaries of performance. This summation highlights the consequence of resistance from boards, senior executives and athletes. Planning, resources and support are discussed as critical areas to enable change while athlete buy-in in the coaching environment is presented as essential!

My account of high performance is very brief compared with the enormity of detail required to facilitate an elite coaching program. The experiences I have managed highlight the significance of planning, structure and staff models that may be compromised by the lack of understanding applied to high performance. Consequently, leadership is presented as a responsible position in the control and maintenance of appropriate high-performance practice.

# CHAPTER 9

# Implications of Change

This chapter is presented where failure to change challenges organisations and an athlete's professionalism.

The tools of change such as reviews, evaluations or assessment are often considered negative when change is considered. Feelings of trepidation and anxiety result on the basis of being measured. So, how difficult is it to implement change?

Many of my professional appointments have dealt with the implementation, the maintenance or the consequences of change. The process of change is fundamental to improving the methods and technologies of the operation to keep pace with best practice and competitors! Scheduled audits and assessments provide invaluable information for staff on the operation's processes and modelling that will keep your program contemporary. Change at this level is as important to the business as its brand is to marketability.

The examples I provide in this chapter about change and its consequences provide insight to the dilemma facing businesses that do not embrace change. Many of my references relate to the individual as a product of the organisation where culture and values are questioned in the context of performance, role responsibilities and ownership of outcomes. The case presented is of an organisation and its standards to challenge behaviour as a necessary step to keep pace with the demands of professionalism.

The following chapter is an account of working with the Glasgow Warriors Rugby Union. At the time (2003), the Scottish Rugby Union (SRU) was experiencing off-field dramas with the domestic game while the provincial teams were also performing poorly in their respective professional competitions. Change was inevitable.

The SRU had a centralised model with franchises owned by the governing body, and they were competing in European and Celtic leagues. As well as working for Glasgow as assistant coach, I was employed by the SRU to manage its high-performance program, which included a specialist coaching role (defence coach) with the national squad.

## Setting the Scene

Head Coach Kiwi Searancke had coached at the highest levels of the game in New Zealand prior to his appointment with the Glasgow Warriors. Articulate and controlled as a coach, his experience was desperately needed at the club. It was sad when he was dismissed in the initial year of his tenure, largely due to an underachieving squad.

Kiwi was an intuitive, strategic and personable coach and a leader of men. I was fortunate to have him as a friend. It was unfortunate that his coaching expertise became compromised as we questioned Glasgow's sense of professionalism. The confrontation between coaching philosophy and athletes was designed to challenge performance standards and, ultimately, incite change.

From my observation, the organisation had conflicted ideals of culture and standards required for a professional franchise. As a by-product, we (the organisation) suffered from a neglected model of operation whereby athletes lacked responsibility and ownership of performance. This period became a lesson about working in a dysfunctional environment rather than coaching a professional rugby team. Everywhere we turned there were issues, be it player recruitment and budgeting, facility upgrades or a misfiring team.

- Performance

As a professional rugby organisation, we have a responsibility to enable peak performance. Providing a platform of success requires a "whole organisation" approach in challenging its own business ethics and goals as an accepted practice. From a coaching perspective, we accept responsibility for failing at several junctures including not building the knowledge and essence of culture and standards. This does not exonerate the organisation or the athletes but merely highlights that the path to excellence is a journey which requires all to be actively aligned.

There were many contributing factors to our mixed results, the eventual demise of our coaching structure and our failure to reinvigorate the club's rugby. Regardless of the issues surrounding the club, as professional coaches, we accept the responsibility of moulding a squad to compete and perform consistently week to week.

Our performances were capable, but we did not have the resolve or consistency necessary to contain the heavyweights of European rugby. We did reach the semi-final of the Celtic League, which underlined the talent in the squad and also highlighted our inability to sustain intense physical battles — a necessary element when competing in the European Cup.

Our performances could best be described as underachieving, which may have been a reflection on the organisation's resources. This squad had talent, experience and flair but lacked the resilience to compete for lengthy periods. Physically, the athlete was compromised by non-rugby specific functional training methods and we had hoped we could resolve inconsistent performances by addressing this immediately.

- Pushback

As staff, we attempted to address this area by searching for an appropriate solution; this included consultation with senior players and club executives to support our recommendations, including an overhaul of recruitment and the player roster. It was sad then for the players to pre-empt our changes by going to the media and the SRU with their concerns. The need for change should have been supported by the SRU executive, but instead it ignored our proposals.

As expected, the athletes felt challenged when change in our approach and demand for a more professional attitude were presented. Our intent was to gain player approval of our proposed changes as much as the senior executive — this was to be a holistic approach to introducing a renewed path to our program.

If we were to be successful as an organisation, our desire to be the best had to be complemented with challenging our business ethic and approach to professionalism. This change was for both short- and long-term benefit.

No changes were made, and performance continued to suffer.

The internal discontent with the proposed changes kickstarted many of the ensuing issues throughout the competitive season. It is sad to think that an introduction of improved standards to compete more effectively at a professional level would result in a mini revolt by the athletes.

Generally, there was a lack of understanding around compliance and appropriate performance standards as well as a lack of responsibility by the athletes to support such measures. Ultimately, they were failing themselves as professional athletes while the national system was inadvertently supporting these standards.

From a high-performance perspective, the system lacked the maturity to self-assess that is demanded of high-achieving sports organisations. This could be seen in senior leaders in the squad who struggled to adapt to the cultural changes that we were ushering in. It was critical that our senior playing group take ownership and facilitate the staff's challenges. This challenge was never taken up and, upon reflection, staff, athletes and executives were never aligned in principle to make change.

- Synopsis

The coaches failed because we lifted the bar of expectation too quickly instead of transitioning those expectations over a longer period. We acknowledged this as an issue but coping in an elite competition was more important than waiting for the squad to adjust to change. In hindsight, it was a catch-22, but we could have managed this process better.

Conversely, our depth of talent was good enough, while key positions were of a national standard. However, we lacked a team culture attuned to the significance of self-assessment for achieving performance-driven outcomes — an invaluable tool to facilitate change.

If our proposals were to be adopted, significant changes to the business culture would have been necessary. Arguably, at Glasgow sub-standard performance was accepted while there was a level of acceptance encouraged and used as a motivation for performance — that is, a non-challenging, non-threatening environment where there was no self-appraisal or desire to challenge their potential! It could be argued that our role as a coaching staff was to realise their potential, but we failed in our approach, delivery or control of the need for change.

When we set about identifying the areas for change, both players and staff were consulted and challenged. All agreed that the dynamic between coaching and support staff needed to be consistent in standards, methodology and processes to drive successful team performance.

## Aligned

Our coaching structure was a simplistic model with the regular fitness, medical and support staff driven by three specialist coaches, all professionally experienced at the highest levels of the game. At some level we were aligned to the organisation's end goal of building a successful squad.

Our game philosophy was physically very demanding and required a strong commitment to challenging the boundaries of mental toughness and individual performance. This strategy would, ironically, contribute to many players being ill-equipped to deliver the style of game we were promoting — a complete oversight from a coaching perspective.

While the staff adopted the philosophy, the athletes struggled to deliver. As the issues surfaced from substandard performances, the athletes closed ranks while staff continued to challenge their performances, thereby leading to constant philosophical debates.

- "Buy-in"

Key considerations in achieving buy-in include an aligned understanding of intelligence and skill level and the ability to convert learning to competitive performance. Our coaching philosophies, styles and vision were conveyed in a deliberate and planned manner, while expectations were clearly set through group and individual mapping sessions. The cycle below sets out the mapping process that had four critical aspects:

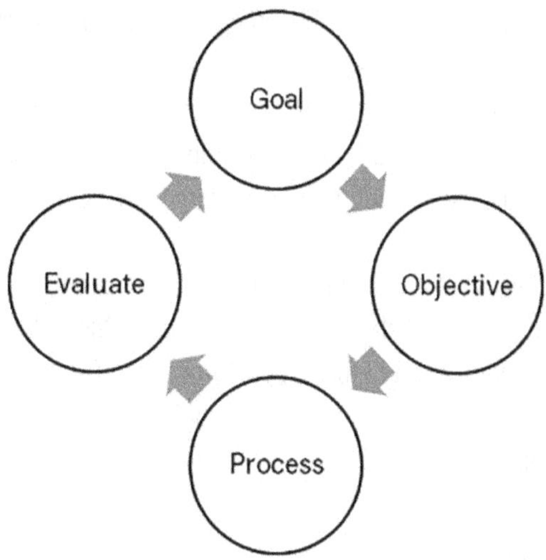


- Goal(s) were aligned initially as a group before devolving those discussions to various levels (i.e., position and individual levels). The stepped process included discussion around how to set goals, what it means and why we do it.
- Objectives were determined for those main elements of peak performance to reach position or individual goals. Objectives are then isolated and broken down into achievable tasks inside key areas of development. For example, game analysis, core skills and fitness.
- Underpinning set objectives are "processes" (i.e., critical aspects determined as essential for reaching set objectives).
- This process is never complete. Evaluations ensure goals, objectives and processors remain valid in the context of team, position or aspiration.

We found that this approach was confrontational, particularly when discussing team accountability (i.e., measuring self-performance). It was a totally new concept to this group and we certainly underestimated the lack of buy-in from the players in this respect. From my perspective, inadequate education and support influenced the lack of buy-in.

Ironically, the changes we had designed and introduced came from a collaborative approach between players, staff and coaches. The changes were designed to challenge process and performance. What we had not accounted for was the extent of the damage an existing and conflicted culture would have on promoting a new vision for the club.

We did, however, have many players strongly advocating change, but too many of the more established athletes controlled the balance of power. As noted, as a staff we had little support from the SRU once change was opposed by the Glasgow executive as being a proposition that was too difficult to achieve.

- Rugby Intelligence

This is often discussed in the context of the ability of our game managers to deliver the game plan. This was an area in which we failed dismally as a coaching group because we misread player experience and their ability to execute and deliver our game strategies. Our match plans required players who could execute strategies under pressure and recognise default systems when challenged.

When performances were questioned, the players became negative and insular within the group and reacted poorly when offered constructive analysis. Considering that feedback is used to improve performance, we were amazed at the inability to accept this facet in their routine as professional rugby players. It's no secret that those who accept constructive criticism generally succeed. Our playing group lacked the maturity to have their performance challenged. Did we manage this process effectively? I would have to say no. Their knowledge of using analysis and those processes including evaluation and correction was poor, at best.

## Critical Factors

In isolation, we had capable players in key positions, but critical moments in games demand precise decision-making and skill selection, which is where we failed consistently as a team. The demands of the game plans affected the ability of our players to apply themselves as needed in clutch moments.

Critical factors were acknowledged and considered in our planning, but this led to further disharmony in our squad:

- The ability to adapt under pressure and deliver a skill with accuracy, control and power is derived from many hours of situational learning. At Glasgow, we found an environment where skill was rehearsed with inappropriate match pressure or lacked the regularity that would enable the skill to be transferred in match time (our preseason training was also hindered by a squad that was not in optimal physical condition).
- We introduced appropriate training schedules that would ensure individual and positional skills were being rehearsed with both quality and pressure (opposed) scenarios.
- It was critical that the opposed skill sessions had been previously neglected and, as a result, our physical approach to training was met with strong opposition.
- As a coaching group, we knew we would get minimal change, but we were negligent by not adopting appropriate training methods. Keeping the status quo was not an option for us.

## Applied Learning

There was no one answer to this dilemma that faced our squad and staff. We knew we had to prepare the players appropriately as rugby professionals, but the steps required would need to be transitioned over years — not months.

It was another catch-22 because time was not on our side and we could not neglect the obvious changes in our training approach that were needed to improve the team. As a staff, we bit the bullet and implemented plans to accommodate the immediate needs of professional rugby.

As expected, the players struggled to adapt to train or play under this volume of work, not to mention the pressure of the changes we were demanding of their attitude shift.

Applied learning certainly was not a new concept! We unearthed a professional program that had neglected to educate, support or manage the players to a point at which their understanding was commensurate with the competition's demands.

**Lessons**

The remodelling process we undertook at Glasgow collided at many key junctures, none more so than the introduction of higher performance standards. Consequently, the education process to introduce change was a massive undertaking, one we misread from a coaching standpoint. There are many areas that needed to be considered (i.e., structure, culture and operation) before change was considered the norm in practice.

It is critical to assess your operation and staff members for opinions and views before making change. Although this aspect was partially addressed, the depth of detail required was neglected, which was an oversight on our part. Inheriting staff, which was the case at Glasgow, presented its own challenges, specifically their perception of existing culture and those we were to support for our vision. Although discussed, we lacked the detail to completely align operation, staff and athlete.

As a coaching staff, juggling multiple balls is common and a fundamental skill that will enable you to perform your role effectively. Balancing inherited staff on top of building your program will always be a major issue when change is imminent.

- Expectations

Implementing new programs requires a conviction to owning the path of expectation, success and failure. We had built the program in a collaborative manner (to a point), but our planning did not include how to manage failure or how the players would deal with the emotional challenge of long-term pain (i.e., inconsistent performance) for sustained success, which is what we were asking of them.

Change has its benefits, but there is also a need to assess the players' and staff members' current understanding of the pace of change. We acknowledged (retrospectively) that we changed too much too soon, even though we had included a transitioning period. We had not planned for the lack of organisational support or the implications of poor buy-in by the players.

- Stakeholders

This was arguably our greatest downfall as a staffing body. When you decide to make changes, which is generally accepted as a given when new coaches are appointed, consider the potential implications for change (risk management). Stakeholders are those persons or bodies that will assist, manage or facilitate change within your system.

Our appointment as a staffing body was widely heralded as what was needed at Glasgow to reinvigorate and professionalise the organisation. Somewhere along the path of change we lost our supporter base, including the media, the board and the governing body. The program demanded change, which was acknowledged by the SRU, but it was sad to be left to stand alone when our planning became unstuck. Accountability, standards and culture collided in many areas during this tenure, while education of performance appraisal, self-evaluation techniques and use of analysis were critical coaching oversights.

Summary by Cameron Blades (former NSW Waratahs, Glasgow Warriors and Wallaby player)

*Steve sums up the issues of change and identifies the main areas and the challenges faced by the Glasgow Warriors coaching staff. As a player at the time, we would all agree that we underperformed and certainly would have benefited from collective "buy-in" as a coaching, playing and management group — something I have now learnt is essential for a professional coach.*

*By the time I was playing for Glasgow, I had been exposed to many different coaching styles and included two World Cup-winning coaches. As a coach in waiting, I was consciously studying Glasgow's coaching style that as an experienced player raised several concerns:*

- *There was an apparent strained relationship between players and coaches that led to a lack of mutual trust*
- *The environment was mentally and physically tough but lacked a sense of enjoyment*
- *Some players felt unfairly treated, which led to team disharmony and inconsistent performance*

*From my observation, some players felt challenged when provided with performance feedback; or they did not respect the opinion of the coaches. With respect: Glasgow's head coach (Kiwi Serancke) was perhaps a reflection of the many challenges faced by the club and playing group. He appeared conflicted in many ways and at times reverted to behaviours that upset the players. As a consequence, the playing squad had lost the respect and challenged the proposed philosophical, performance and cultural changes.*

*Although they were an experienced coaching staff, they had no history together, which only further exacerbated the task of ushering in changes.*

*In saying that, ultimately as a playing group we did not display a "growth mindset" or accept (cultural) change.*

**Postscript by Michael Byrne** (professional rugby coach – former Wallabies, All Blacks, Scotland, Japan; former AFL Premiership winner)

*Leadership from the governing body is necessary to elicit change in the way athletes perform and conduct themselves in everyday life. Failure of an organisation to do so is abdicating responsibility. Steve's discussion has highlighted the importance to embrace change but also the need to be enabled from "top to bottom" (i.e., governing body, club and athlete). At this time, I may add, professional rugby in Europe was still in its infancy. This created its own issues where athletes and coaches were adjusting to the rigours and demands of professionalism — which could account for the indifference by Glasgow players to accept the need for change.*

*As Scotland's national assistant coach, my role was to visit professional franchises (i.e., Glasgow, Edinburgh and Borders) for skill development programs. I always enjoyed my visits to Glasgow as the environment was challenging, with an intent to improve and to "get better." The coaches were working hard to increase the standard and level of preparation to support a competitive team on the world stage. Playing an active part in facilitating change with Glasgow's coaches, I observed several key issues:*

- *Significantly, professionalising the system was a major undertaking as a relatively new concept that encountered resistance from several senior players. Learning, as a precursor to change, was challenged where the younger athletes were more accepting while the "aging" athlete was less likely to accept change.*
- *The perception was that another couple of foreign coaches were challenging "our culture and the way it's always been"; this was a major obstacle for change. Although change was being ushered in by senior coaches, their expertise and experience meant little in the scheme of accepting new standards.*

- *The players' idea of being "professional" meant being paid a good size wage — an indication of the immaturity of the organisation and the athletes' attitudes. The standard players had become accustomed to was now being challenged on the premise of working harder every day to get better. Physical standards, skill levels and tactical prowess were all being challenged as a platform to enable a consistently high performing elite team — a fact not realised by this group.*

*In forty-three years of professional sport as an elite athlete and now high-performance coach, I am convinced a professional system built on a "whole of organisation" approach will drive the players to achieve; a significant factor I feel, overlooked by the Scottish Rugby Union and Glasgow Warriors.*

# CHAPTER 10

# High Performance

Commitment to detail is necessary if excellence is to be achieved. As a high-performance coach, detail is king.

The term high performance (HP) continues to be part of our language in sport, whether referring to talented youth, development programs or the support of professional athletes.

Over the many years I have been involved in professional sport, I have witnessed the mechanisation of high performance driven back into our sporting framework to our junior athletes, often to the detriment of individual development as elite sports look to fast-track our talented youth.

In this chapter, I discuss my experience of high performance in professional rugby and how excellence is achieved through the application of detailed and supported systems. My discussion references the applications that have evolved in professional coaching. Specifically, clarity, precision of operation and change management are discussed as essential to achieving HP practices.

## Defining HP

My definition of HP refers to how we educate, build and guide the development of our best, most talented athletes while describing the use of coaching, psychology and physical development as key components to the individual's performance.

While the evolution of the term HP has developed in the resourcing of our elite programs, I have found common factors that drive HP, such as attention to detail, elevated performance demands on program intent, and the constant challenge of the supporting processes all being geared toward building success. This resourced, process-driven approach provides the key to understanding HP, its application and the influence on performance outcomes.

Resourcing HP has played a critical part in its application, particularly in the expansion of elite pathway systems. This discussion of applied HP principles with our talented youth is a debate on its own, considering the physical and psychological challenges of maturation.

My descriptions of HP have been shaped by my experiences as an elite coach from an applied perspective, specifically the search for performance excellence. The following HP references are not qualified by science but are merely anecdotal observations from my three decades of working in high-performance sport.

### Understanding HP

From the detail comes process. HP demands that staff are working systematically to improve their methods and expectations of performance. Continuous improvement will occur if staff appreciate that actively challenging the system will provide the focus for precision.

My understanding of HP is driven by how best to use the tools that are available to improve and capture excellence in performance. Simply put, it is about how we perceive and achieve peak performance by validating it through competing against the best. As coaches, how we drive individuals and teams to realise next level performance through the measure of consistency is primary to achieving HP alignment between coach and squad.

At an individual level, every element of my coaching experience is driven by process, which enables efficiency and effectiveness of each action. This means that every action is performed with the attainment of quality in mind. Each specific moment, individual or team action is measured against predetermined outcomes that collectively provide the basis for improvement, with an intent to achieve consistency of performance. For this reason, a generic explanation of HP becomes challenging due to the complexity, diversity and nature of each environment.

All functions of HP require supporting detail that ultimately contributes to a positive outcome; neglect any one aspect, and the result may be conflicted or lost. The explanations of HP are many and varied, and the need for detailed analysis within your environment to support continuous improvement must remain a focus.

## Building an HP System

Mention high performance and thinking generally aligns with the science of sport in respect to athletic development and well-being. These are just two components of the many disciplines within HP that contribute to the coach being able to decipher and determine what actions are to be taken.

In the following section, I have identified four key areas that I consider to be fundamental to building an HP environment with consideration for an end goal, resources and continuous improvement. I have used various experiences to provide context to their relationship with high performance.

1.    Clarity, Compromise and Leaders

- Clarity

Part of planning is setting measures that allow the organisation a standard of operation commensurate with resources and deliverables. Too often, organisational goals are clouded by governance models conflicted by operational jargon, inadequate structure, inexperienced staff, or lack of the detailed planning required for elite environments.

Clarity is essential where staff delineation and performance process drive (winning) outcomes. Essentially, clear vision must support athlete, coach and staff excellence.

- Compromise

There is a simple analogy and a commonly spoken reference in high-performance sport: never give in. For me, giving in to compromise, or giving an inch, signals the intent to surrender an advantage.

Elite sport demands respect for detail — compromise and you will fail. Accepting mediocrity will derail the operation. When dealing with high-achieving athletes, winning drives their existence. By default, the organisation and its culture need alignment where excellence is reflected in staff (high achievers), planning (strategic intent) and vision for sustained excellence (building a legacy).

- Leaders

The character of an HP leader is unmistakeable where achieving excellence drives their career. I see the same traits in high-achieving athletes. Elite sport is unforgiving both mentally and physically and demands strong, robust and resilient leaders.

Working in elite sport is not for everyone! High performance is not for the "9-5" worker. The job demands long days that often sacrifice family and social pursuits. Successful organisations have strong leaders who employ like-minded people who have vision and sport intellect and who constantly strive for excellence. HP environments demand like-minded persons who are driven to succeed.

The drive for success must have a leader with resolve who challenges the pursuit of excellence while enabling staff to develop and lead. Successful organisations I have worked in have leaders that surround themselves with like-minded staff who can work independently with self-confidence and expertise. They are generally high-achieving individuals who promote a value system that demands aligned principles with common practice, standards and a "will to win."

2.  Expert staffing, planning and responsibility

- Expert Staffing

Any form of compromise will challenge performance. That is, an elite athlete with poor coaching will be disadvantaged; so too will an organisation with sub-standard operations or unqualified staff. When discussing staff support in HP environments, it is often overlooked as insignificant. As a manager, this may require making a call on staff competency, which can be difficult. But any form of compromise (e.g., inappropriate levels of athlete support) will harm performance and success.

Although the reach of HP has expanded, so has the mindset of what elite performance is! It has softened to a point where junior development is referred to as "elite" or "high performance." That is a discussion of its own but an indication of the changing perception of HP.

High-performance settings will have their visions, plans and structures, but if you want success at the highest levels of sport, employ those who have experienced success, who have driven challenging environments and who have like-minded philosophies and a strong desire to win at all costs. Excellence, winning and attainment of goals is having the right people who are working to a common place through common practices. This would appear common considering the challenge of building a high-performing environment that produces winning teams — many of my experiences of failure or not winning are directly related to not being on the same page, being unaligned or lacking a high-achieving operation model.

- Responsibility

As leaders, we operate to standards with business integrity central to workplace deliverables. However, there are instances where this edict is challenged in high-performance sport.

I have seen many executives survive while the coach carries the brunt of failure. Sure, the coach is responsible for delivering a competitive squad, but why blame "middle management" (the head coach) when times get tough?

In some respects, the coach is only as good as the business model and leadership. Generally, a CEO is not in the firing line when things go awry. In team sports such as rugby, the head coach typically becomes the sole owner of poor performance while executives enter a world of political rhetoric that rationalises failure. This statement by no means exonerates the head coach, but with respect, due diligence and responsibility, it starts with organisation executives!

Losing creates all sorts of challenges, not least managing club image. My time at Warrington (Super League, UK) springs to mind as an example of a conflicted leadership impacting performance. As head coach, I was left to front the media's questions that targeted the performance of the whole organisation, while the team's outcomes were only part of the organisation's goals. In many respects, these questions would have been better handled by the chairman or CEO.

High-performance coaching is about results, so losing often requires the media to be managed in a way that provides balance to performance. Simply adding other stories or diverting storylines away from losing can offset media pressure on the team. Taking the spotlight off poor performance may be considered diversionary, but being able to regroup without media pressure provides a more relaxed training environment.

Generally, media responses scheduled by the club are often scripted for the head coach, while executives choose key moments to address the masses, often distancing themselves from the coach and team performance.

The chairman or CEO should absorb the criticism or front the organisation when there is conflict, challenge or disarray to protect the staff and business ideals. From a professional stance I question their leadership and responsibility in times of crisis with equal fortitude rather than the coach carrying all the blame for poor performance.

- Planning

Benjamin Franklin said, "By failing to prepare, you are preparing to fail." The significance of planning at elite levels of sport cannot be understated, and mapping out the direction is common sense. The long-term plan presented during my tenure at Warrington offers an example of issues executives consider when discussing HP.

My plan isolated critical issues of recruitment and retention, which aligned the academy program with community development. This was essential to sustainable success.

Planning included a strong warning to the executive that inconsistent performance would occur while rebuilding and executive resolve would be required. Although a struggle lay ahead, the reliance on overseas imports would only provide short-term savings on player lists!

3.  Executive Commitment to Invest

As a head coach, the board's support is critical to the end goal of consistent, successful performance. In times of crisis, I have repeatedly witnessed the fragility of leadership as linkages between governance, structure and planning fracture.

Modern rugby has moved on markedly at a professional level where, for example, coaching demands vision, fluidity and deliverables that hold your program to account. Accordingly, the board recognising HP as an investment rather than a "consideration" to achieving success is paramount.

Once a strategic intent to success is mapped and financial support is in place, the ability of the organisation to realise its goals will improve as will the scope to hire world-class specialist staff (i.e., sports psychologists, nutritionists, position coaches and analysts) and elite talent, which will increase the chance of sustained success.

- Resources

Today's athletes are tracked by monitors and constant analysis of key performance indicators, while daily well-being and medical screening ensure they are "fit for purpose."

The cost of resourcing an HP unit sits secondary to list-management (i.e., the cost of contracting elite athletes to fit the coach's plans) while rehabilitation services, doctors, nutritionists and world-class training facilities work in tandem with professional staff and elite coaches! Welcome to the world of high performance.

Setting up a high-performance program requires a detailed scanning of the existing environment while investing in support structures to achieve consistent performance and future success.

- Investing in HP

While working as head of academy (Western Force, SANZAR Super Rugby competition, 2016-17), I compared our "point of difference" (i.e., Did we have a winning edge? What made us better than others?) to other competing franchises. The areas I specifically focussed on were talent identification and recruitment strategies. Recruitment and succession planning are key to sustainable success while athlete identification is a specialist skill requiring networks in major national underage competitions, school programs and junior clubs at domestic and international levels.

My initial assessment concluded that neither talent identification nor recruitment were supported strategically or financed appropriately for an elite rugby environment. This was why we needed to buy athletes into the franchise rather than invest internally to develop the players and pathway systems.

Talent and athlete succession provide indicators to effectiveness while definable systems and the appropriate level of investment are critical for sustained success. The Western Force suffered from a lack of investment in the key systems of staff modelling, aligned development and the athlete-centred approach, which meant they couldn't produce elite athletes as well as other franchises. This is a contributing factor to the club's low rankings and the reason they only once challenged for finals contention in a twelve-year history.

Most critically, the operation, although under-resourced at critical points of HP (i.e., the academy model, scouting or a systematic approach to recruitment) lacked a coherent or productive program.

- Talent

Central to a franchise's existence is the production of elite players, while talent identification and retention of its best products should be a derivative of the organisation's HP unit. Too often recruitment can be misinterpreted at professional levels of sport where available funding predetermines the mindset of athlete investment and, consequently, staff modelling. Buying available talent to fill immediate gaps is a "hit and miss" approach promoting a false economy that ultimately compromises consistency and sustainability.

At the elite level the aim is simple: remain competitive on and off the field and invest appropriately to remain sustainable. To remain competitively investing in (young) talent to support competitive squads is a fundamental element in building for the future. Strategic intent to be the best requires investment in the club's future, which invariably lays within its talent roster and essential recruitment planning.

- List Management

Managing player lists must be accompanied by high standards of organisational commitment to winning, competitiveness and consistency of performance.

For example, while at Melbourne Storm (NRL), we deliberately regulated the movement of marquee athletes while securing second and third tier players in our talent pool. This enabled a depth of talent to call on for those vulnerable positions while also operating long-term succession.

Our feeder club at the time (Northern Suburbs, Queensland Rugby League) provided a good standard of competition for players and a testing ground for our development players. This approach of providing "competition and development" are two important cogs for recruitment. Knowing who you sign is one element, while investment into your system with appropriate resources is the underlying key to producing consistently high calibre, elite players.

Recruitment, retention and talent identification processes are central to success. Mapping a process-driven program that outlines acceptable and unacceptable measures of success is fundamental for sustainability. Tasks that underpin those processes are designed to capture the commitment of the organisation and keep pace with HP fundamentals that unlock success.

4.    Continuous Improvement

Continual improvement is accepting that the system and process are perpetually in a state of flux because of the ever-changing demands of elite performance. Athletes, staff and functions must be aligned to keep pace with the threat of inconsistent performance. Alignment will ensure there is consistent, targeted support, which enables development.

As a coach, some functions are naturally directed toward the development of individual performance in training and competition. You must consider a process of review that, ultimately, will target the improvement of supporting programs.

For many years I have used a process that guides and questions specific elements of both rugby performance and supporting operation. This process can be broken into key elements:

- *Leadership programs* that support the development of leaders
- *Communication* and use of consistent terminology across the coaching program
- Facility and scheduling processes that support the *physical environment*
- *Core planning* of athletic, skill, position-specific and correction processes
- *Strategic development* for game specific programs (i.e., unit, offense and defense programs)
- Psychological and *performance profiling* supporting individual development
- Performance assessment (analysis) and processes to educate and support *athlete education*

- Determine *organisation targets* and key milestones to track long-term performance

The organisation's purpose is defined by facilitating a collaborative and transparent view to building a platform for improvement and stepped change. This process is underpinned by feedback with consideration to staff and athlete development. There are many ways to capture this information, such as:

- Informal and formal learning platforms that ensure your athletes are continually enabled.
- Supported analysis that challenges or validates performance.
- Performance appraisals for staff and athletes to create continuous development.
- Staff reporting utilised as a mechanism to present new ideas.
- Action plan for change.

### Lessons

Understanding your objectives and tasks and how they are aligned to expectations leads to the path of excellence. As a professional coach, adopting high-performance principles must be considered an accepted practice to realise success. Experience reflects the challenges that confront high-performance initiatives.

## Know Your Purpose

To set your journey on the road to success is to know the principles, boundaries and functions of high performance. Too often, HP is miscalculated on the premise that operations and staff are working toward agreed objectives only to find their interpretations of the premise do not align. Winning at the elite level of the sport requires 360 degrees of commitment to ensure HP principles drive actions and behaviours that underpin success. The ability and success of your business is driven by a commitment to achieving excellence through intentional planning and aligned purpose.

- Where Do You Stand?

Coaching at the elite level requires strong resolve with the ability to manage direction and change. Your philosophy, process and system will come under scrutiny. Having confidence and being forthright and transparent with your employer and stakeholders is fundamental for professional integrity and longevity. Stating your position to establish a working relationship should be backed by planning, expectations and the goals of your tenure. As mentioned, many factors will determine the stability of your position, not least the organisation's expectation of winning.

To walk away knowing your integrity and work practices remain intact is more important than any success. I have been fortunate to work in successful organisations that understand value, integrity and respect is essential for success.

- Add Value and Impact

From a philosophical perspective, contributing to a new coaching appointment in a unique manner can be rewarding and challenging. In high-performance settings I have always been confident to adapt and progress the environment as a leader or a team member. At a professional level, necessary change is encouraged and embraced as part of the organisation's culture. Those environments that remain reluctant to change often struggle to grow or realise their potential. It's true that "You cannot grow unless you are willing to change."

**Postscript by Matt Williams** (former head coach NSW Waratahs, Leinster, Ulster and Scotland national team)

*As Steve rightly observes, much of developing elite coaches' learnings focus on the technical and tactical aspects of their sport.*

*A head coach must be a competent leader of cultural change, organisational unity, and the driver of the absolute necessity for creating the constant growth that is essential to all long-term success in high-performance sport. From experience, these aspects of a coach's education are almost always neglected or underdeveloped.*

*Coaches tend to learn these leadership skills on the job. Many of us carry the scars of our early failings in these areas for the rest of our working lives.*

*There is a lot more to being head coach than a deep knowledge of your sport. Managing people and how they interact within an organisation is as complex and diverse as the people themselves.*

*Added to all of this, Steve correctly observes that the head coach must be the glue that binds the players, staff, CEO and chairperson together as they walk the rocky path of cultural growth as an organisation.*

*This process is never easy. There are hidden pitfalls at every step. The best of intentions can result in catastrophic unintended outcomes.*

*To navigate all of this, positive interpersonal relationships that create trust across all the stakeholders are paramount.*

*The longevity of these key relationships within this environment is always helpful and makes the process easier. With time, trust is improved. Trust empowers the inevitable challenges that arise to be overcome.*

*As a coach, being able to stay around long enough to create those powerful, lasting interpersonal relationships is the tricky part.*

*Steve provides powerful insights into what it takes to stay on course in this essential but not often discussed area of high-performance coaching.*

157

# Chapter 11

# Conclusions

So, what have I achieved in writing this book? The simplicity of my preface is reflected in the many lessons I have presented for the aspiring or experienced coach. My discussion has targeted the "how and what" of coaching to isolate perceived myths, issues and challenges of coaching. Specific experiences have been explained to provide a means to understanding the complexity of managing the coach environment. Themes such as the coach's personality and significance to development; dealing with conflict; managing elite athletes; and the consequences of success and failure in high-performing environments have been discussed to highlight the demands of coaching.

This project was created to explore specific areas of my journey as a professional coach and discuss the reality and implications of those roles. My intention was to present guideposts that contain triggers or precursors to subject matter that is commonplace but not referenced in coaching manuals.

## Coaching is a Journey of Experience

Mentors, education and early appointments are important to the development of a coach. Those early experiences hold the key to decisions and actions that will define you as a coach. They are decisions that can enable or stifle your development or elevate you to heights of elite coaching.

Decisions — right, wrong or indifferent — are to be accepted as learning experiences, which, for me, in many ways provided intrigue and interest that led to a career path as a coach.

Constructively, I have exposed my naivety in early coaching roles to present this is as normal and essential for your development. Accepting that there will be moments of inadequacy, a lack of clarity or the ability to provide solutions is a part of learning and highlights the need for mentors. This area is critical to development.

My early appointments were awkward but provided practical solutions to be an effective coach; a lesson realised many years later. It was my intention to expose these appointments to highlight the many facets of coaching, the varying demands and the challenging dynamic that exists inside the coaching environment. Further, the feeling and intent to "fit in" and be accepted by players and staff is an area that can detract from your role. What became evident was my need to know how I was perceived — an area of wasted time and spent emotions. The key is to identify and be comfortable with who you are, and not to be caught obsessing with "acceptance" as primary to your role as coach.

Your role is simple: to assess and guide the ability of your players and find common goals that lead to victory. I went through long periods in my early development trying to offer unique methods that only complicated the task at hand. At the time that felt "right" but I was neglecting the most important aspect of coaching: the individual and team competency and the development. Build your plans with simplicity in mind and through knowing your group. A very simple message for coaches.

As the apprentice coach, I wanted to communicate the need for exploring the boundaries of delivery. As Peter Ryan (Queensland Reds Rugby defence coach) eluded: being thrown into the deep end allowed for my own way of dealing with situations. From a mentoring perspective this approach provides an opportunity to challenge your own sense of right in what you offer the playing group. This also encouraged ownership and responsibility of work and actions — a big part of being the coach. Accept early opportunities for experience and owning your development.

Another area I found beneficial to personal development was seeking information from related topics that indirectly or directly may assist your coaching. I have found this (study) invaluable to challenge how I go about my work while adding a depth of knowledge to my skill set. This is invaluable, but experience is your saviour.

There were many challenges in my early development, an accepted element to all roles. If I compare the "then and now" and the "how and what" to my coaching skills such as man management and leadership, they are incomparable today. For me, this reflection highlights experience as essential for growth. Those same challenges exist today but my ability to manage is more refined. For example: How I deal with the athlete today is far more complex than as a novice coach thirty years ago. Today I have depth, knowledge and experience to draw upon while yester-year was, in many instances, trial and error. Time and patience are key.

## Elite Coaching Requires Resolve

An aspect often overlooked and not generally expected is the reality that you will be challenged for a myriad of aspects. Coaching the elite is far from easy. The environment in many ways is the same at amateur level but when coaching the best, you are being tested to provide methods that expand the capacity of the athlete, team and outcome. What I have discussed is the enormity and responsibility of coaching our best and becoming proficient at managing that environment. This is complex and demanding.

One of the most diverse and complex areas to manage is the dynamic that exists inside the playing group. Hierarchies — informal and formal — exist, while the coach must acknowledge there is a responsibility to enable this dynamic as part of the team's ability to perform. There is no one way to manage "hierarchy" as each environment is different due to the varying personalities. Some environments require careful and meaningful support while others exist on a seniority that is allocated by the group. The more complex by nature and operation the more challenging for the coach. Part of this dynamic is to truly set out to know the individual — this provides you with armour when issues arise from within.

Being resilient as a coach is a prerequisite, and with experience, your resolve thickens. Selections in particular provide many headaches as you set about finding balance and transparency. No matter how clear or open the selection criteria, there will always be issues — at all levels. The key is to be solid in your convictions, establish and communicate key criterion and be open to being questioned as a matter of process. This is by far one of the most demanding areas of elite coaching as media twist and invariably debate your final selections.

Another aspect that requires conviction is building a model of operation that fits your philosophy. Finding the balance between organisation and your team's goals can determine an appropriate model. As an example: team selections require a defined criterion to ensure a balance of opinion between executive, coach and stakeholder. This is a signal to all coaches.

Constantly challenging your coaching environment provides a means to remain contemporary to the squad's preparation and performance. As a critical aspect, developing mentoring programs to in-service those players who could and will become senior leaders is crucial for squad development. The real test for any coach when discussing player leadership and development is to surrender components of the coach environment to the squad's senior leaders. This enables and develops the designated leaders and ensures your coaching program evolves to a collective ownership model — significant in terms of team buy-in. For the coach this is also a test of your ability to delegate and accept mentoring as key to the squad's harmony.

The demands of coaching the elite and accepting the part they play in your application in preparation and competition must be a goal. At the elite level, recruiting athletes that possess accepting behaviours enables and activates so many other areas as the coach and squad work to achieve a harmonious existence. In many cases this may not be achieved, but it is certainly an ideal to strive for in piecing together a competitive squad.

The respect I hold for the elite rugby athlete is underlined by their willingness to work in extreme physical and mental states. The challenge for the coach is to appreciate the moving pieces inside the pro ranks that will demand your attention. Culture, depleted squad lists or inadequate staff models all have relevance while unity, comradery and collegiate thinking is imperative and should be pursued. This is a massive challenge. To put that in perspective I have experienced only one environment (Melbourne Storm, NRL) in three decades of professional coaching where culture reflected and aligned the whole organisation in the attainment of success, so it's important to be realistic in your aspirations and goals. Winning championships often remains a dream.

## The Philosophical Challenge of Coaching

The challenge to remain true to your philosophy is to recognise experience as your guide. For many of my appointments there have been scenarios that require patience and resilience to modify behaviour and standards. There have been many occasions where my own sense of value has been conflicted as a result of authoritarian forms of leadership, often at the expense of the athlete or team performance.

Organisational conflict will occur (generally) due to poor communication. From experience, this occurs more often from unclear roles, irregular or inconsistent communication channels, or a lack of respect for formal process across the operation. As a result, performance is affected and impacts on athlete morale, staff effectiveness and attainment of goals. Prepare for this situation.

Of significance, honesty, trust and integrity have been integral to my coaching while loyalty holds prominence to my principles. For me, writing about these areas provides a "real" look at what professional coaching can be and has been for me. The challenge of staying honest to your philosophies will remain constant throughout your career as situations arise that test your ability to stay true to your convictions. Coaching is a continuous balancing act between goals, business process and coaching principles all to benefit the player. Lose sight of this and coaching will become clouded. The player's "state" is central to your remit.

What is your priority? Winning at all costs or winning with integrity? If winning is the goal, then does the cost become irrelevant? My philosophy is governed by honesty while winning is but a consequence of an environment underpinned by integrity of operation and performance. I have no desire to jeopardise my beliefs for winning. This is not to denigrate success as this is our ultimate reward, but I will not sacrifice my beliefs.

Professionalism and its worth can be best described as "conflicted." From my experience, each environment has specific traits driven by culture, tradition and history and experienced personalities who lead the organisation. There is much to be said for "whole of organisation" alignment of goals that ensures conflict is marginalised. Success has common and not so common traits while elitism thrives where ego appears critical to winning. In this environment, leadership is represented as strong, inflexible and confined to the process and systems that support success. As a consequence, human emotion, staff care and athlete welfare may become secondary to success.

There is also the side-show to professional sport: the media. The enormity of the media's influence at the professional level cannot be understated. In many cases the media convey a sense of entitlement to know the inner sanctum of the coaching environment. They act as the conscience for the community. I've yet to understand why, but certainly I have experienced the influence of the media and its consequence to performance and tenure. Be aware of the media's impact on your role!

## Continuous Improvement is High Performance

Continuous improvement should be an accepted process in your coaching plan. But many factors will need to be considered. Once identified, positioning those changes requires time for adjustment and recognition by the squad as an accepted standard. Critically, continuous education of key strategies for change should be a planning consideration to achieve buy-in.

"Change" has been presented as necessary to keep your environment at its peak. Generally speaking, when change is discussed the response can be conflicted and often represented by discomfort and concern. While I am an advocate for continuous improvement, change should not occur as a result of a whim. Change at the elite level of rugby should be strategic and generated by internal reviews and a process that should alleviate the concerns of the organisation (i.e., by discussing the process and benefit).

Aligned organisations, strategic intent and individual goals should be an end goal for elite environments. At stages, the attainment of an aligned organisation may seem to be an ideal, but it is certainly achievable if continuous improvement is facilitated in a manner that is inclusive, rewarding and outcome driven. For high-performance settings this thinking should be non-negotiable.

There are many factors that implicate change, but none more so than challenging culture (i.e., performance and standards). Although searching for improved performance, athletes will naturally feel challenged when their standards are threatened. How you present this information to the athletes is crucial for acceptance and for change to take place. These moments are not about science but more about how improvement can be made through an attitude shift. As a coach, this is as challenging a task as you will face.

High performance is such an overused term. My attempt to define high performance fell short of my expectations in this book. What I have achieved is to identify the key mechanisations that underpin and drive high performance such as: resources, astute leaders, high achieving staff and elite coaches, and a depth of athletes to draw upon. Not an easy configuration. Compromising these essential areas of high performance will lead to inconsistent performance or failure to achieve outcomes.

- A Final Word

My book is a collection of themes designed to capture the emotions, philosophies and challenges of coaching. I have presented an account of what is to be expected during your journey as a professional coach that I hope will provide a guide to your development. Certainly, the role of coach isn't for everyone and finding your niche is incredibly important. By that I mean there are many roles that can service your passion.

From a personal perspective, this book has provided an opportunity to speak with past players and coaches, which has been enlightening in many respects. Introspectively we all have our ideas on how we are perceived as coaches and people. This exercise has challenged me to self-reflect, a process that has revealed the importance of acknowledging failed experiences as necessary for owning your decisions and actions.

The occasions of second-guessing decisions still remain with me, but I've now accepted this as part of the dynamic of coaching. Having doubt isn't to be confused with a personality flaw, but rather as an acknowledgment to decisions made through tough periods in our careers that sometimes fail. This is a reality of coaching.

The book's themes and lessons reflect on experiences that will provide reflective lessons for coaching while revealing the emotional rollercoaster of professional coaching. I am confident my shared experiences will benefit you in your journey as a coach.

Coaching is truly a complex workplace.